FTCE
English 6-12
Practice Questions

T0289638

Mometrix
TEST PREPARATION

DEAR FUTURE EXAM SUCCESS STORY

First of all, **THANK YOU** for purchasing Mometrix study materials!

Second, congratulations! You are one of the few determined test-takers who are committed to doing whatever it takes to excel on your exam. **You have come to the right place.** We developed these practice tests with one goal in mind: to deliver you the best possible approximation of the questions you will see on test day.

Standardized testing is one of the biggest obstacles on your road to success, which only increases the importance of doing well in the high-pressure, high-stakes environment of test day. Your results on this test could have a significant impact on your future, and these practice tests will give you the repetitions you need to build your familiarity and confidence with the test content and format to help you achieve your full potential on test day.

Your success is our success

We would love to hear from you! If you would like to share the story of your exam success or if you have any questions or comments in regard to our products, please contact us at **800-673-8175** or **support@mometrix.com**.

Thanks again for your business and we wish you continued success!

Sincerely,
The Mometrix Test Preparation Team

TABLE OF CONTENTS

Practice Test #1

1. Which of the following authors was a 19th-century British novelist and short-story writer?

 a. O. Henry
 b. Charles Dickens
 c. Herman Melville
 d. Nathaniel Hawthorne

2. Of the following classic works, which one is NOT an epic poem?

 a. *Beowulf*
 b. *The Odyssey*
 c. *Divine Comedy*
 d. *The Decameron*

3. Placing literature in historical context, which of the following statements is true?

 a. William Shakespeare published *Hamlet* before the first American colony was made.
 b. Geoffrey Chaucer wrote *The Canterbury Tales* after Columbus visited the Americas.
 c. John Milton published *Paradise Lost* before Charles II's return to the English throne.
 d. James Joyce wrote *Finnegans Wake* and Richard Wright wrote *Native Son* after WWII.

4. Which of these American literary classics reflects the Civil War in its setting?

 a. *The Adventures of Tom Sawyer* by Mark Twain
 b. *Uncle Tom's Cabin* by Harriet Beecher Stowe
 c. *Little Women* by Louisa May Alcott
 d. *Moby-Dick* by Herman Melville

5. What is the correct terminology for a group of related ideas, expressed in multiple lines of text, and separated from other such groups by spaces, in the genre of poetry?

 a. Verse
 b. Stanza
 c. Refrain
 d. Paragraph

6. Which poetic form is characterized by three lines in free verse, always totaling 17 syllables, with each line frequently having five, seven, and five syllables respectively, and concisely but vividly conveying the experience of an image, scene, and/or moment?

 a. Haiku
 b. Ballad
 c. Sonnet
 d. Limerick

7. Within the genre of poetry, poems in which form are the shortest and easiest to remember?

 a. Odes
 b. Epics
 c. Elegies
 d. Epigrams

1

8. Within the novelistic genre, the novel of manners is a form identifiable by which of the following characteristics?

    a. Language individually personalized for each character or situation
    b. The written expressions and exploration of powerful emotions
    c. Symbolically representing some established, secure social order
    d. Describing society without defining any of its codes of behavior

9. Which of the following novels is typically considered the first example of the *Bildungsroman?*

    a. *Wilhelm Meister's Apprenticeship* by Johann Wolfgang von Goethe
    b. *The Sorrows of Young Werther* by Johann Wolfgang von Goethe
    c. *Great Expectations* by Charles Dickens
    d. *David Copperfield* by Charles Dickens

10. Of the following, which technique is NOT commonly shared by both satire and realism?

    a. Writing that utilizes a serious tone
    b. Exaggerating situations and ideas
    c. Portraying irony in situations
    d. Writing vernacular dialogue

11. Which of the following use(s) figurative meaning rather than literal meaning?

    a. The willow tree has long branches that trail.
    b. The willow tree's leaves look like teardrops.
    c. The willow tree is weeping into the stream.
    d. Options (b) and (c) are figurative, while (a) is literal.

12. In his short story "The Tell-Tale Heart" (1843), Edgar Allan Poe writes in the main character's narration, "How, then, am I mad? Harken! and observe how healthily—how calmly I can tell you the whole story... Now this is the point. You fancy me mad. Madmen know nothing. But you should have seen *me*. You should have seen how wisely I proceeded — with what caution — with what foresight — with what dissimulation I went to work! I was never kinder to the old man than during the whole week before I killed him." What did Poe want readers to infer from this text?

    a. That the character is sane
    b. That the character is mad
    c. That the character is evil
    d. That (a) and (c) are true, not (b)

Refer to the following for questions 13 - 16:

> It was the best of times, it was the worst of times, it was the age of wisdom, it was the age of foolishness, it was the epoch of belief, it was the epoch of incredulity, it was the season of Light, it was the season of Darkness, it was the spring of hope, it was the winter of despair, we had everything before us, we had nothing before us, we were all going direct to heaven, we were all going direct the other way – in short, the period was so far like the present period, that some of its noisiest authorities insisted on its being received, for good or for evil, in the superlative degree of comparison only.

> From *A Tale of Two Cities* by Charles Dickens (1859)

13. Which best expresses one main idea that Dickens wanted readers to realize from this introduction?
   a.   That everything could seem to be best or worst according to individual perceptions
   b.   That the past described was so identical to the present they were indistinguishable
   c.   That the past and present both had equal balances of good/light and evil/darkness
   d.   That the extremities of good and bad described were imagined by the "authorities"

14. Of the following statements, which accurately describe(s) textual evidence of Dickens's techniques and their effects?
   a.   The even rhythm and use of anaphora reinforce the ideas of equal and opposing forces.
   b.   The presentation of multiple opposites introduces a main "doubles" motif and structure.
   c.   The author's use of anastrophe together with rhythm emphasizes contrasting opposites.
   d.   The statements in (a) and (b) are both accurate, but the statement in (c) makes an error.

15. Among the following, which pair most represents the use of figurative meanings?
   a.   Wisdom and foolishness
   b.   Belief and incredulity
   c.   Light and darkness
   d.   Hope and despair

16. From reading only this introductory paragraph, what can readers infer about this novel overall?
   a.   That the story may include equal proportions of positives and negatives
   b.   That the story may include a greater proportion of negatives than positives
   c.   That the story may include a greater proportion of positives than negatives
   d.   That the story may include nothing readers can infer from just this beginning

17. Which of these best represents a main theme in William Shakespeare's *Romeo and Juliet*?
   a.   Teenage love will always lead to tragedy.
   b.   Individuals defying society may be fatal.
   c.   Love and violence are unrelated entities.
   d.   Fate does not control those who defy it.

18. A prominent theme in Victor Hugo's *Les Misérables* may be described how?

    a. The importance of love and compassion for others
    b. The success of the French Revolution with society
    c. The Revolution's end to the class system in France
    d. The futility of loving and having compassion for others

19. In Edgar Allan Poe's story *The Tell-Tale Heart,* which of the following is NOT a way in which he develops the theme of madness and paranoia?

    a. The narrator's admission of insanity
    b. The narrator's denial of his insanity
    c. The narrator's fixation on the "eye"
    d. The narrator's projection of sound

20. Which of these defines a universal theme found in both Genesis in the Old Testament and the Quran, as well as the Epic of Gilgamesh?

    a. God's destruction of people for their wicked behavior
    b. God's instruction to one man to build a ship to survive
    c. Man's sending out a bird after the flood to test things
    d. Man's whole population destroyed except on an ark

21. One universal theme related to the following characters can best be described how?

    a. In Greek mythology, Icarus went too far; Prometheus did not go far enough.
    b. In Genesis, Adam and Eve went too far; in *The Old Man and the Sea,* Santiago did not.
    c. In these stories, Icarus and Prometheus did not go far enough; the others all went too far.
    d. Adam and Eve and Prometheus went too far with knowledge; the others went too far out.

22. In which of the following literary works is the first-person narrative told by the main character?

    a. *Sherlock Holmes* by Sir Arthur Conan Doyle
    b. *The Tell-Tale Heart* by Edgar Allan Poe
    c. *Gulliver's Travels* by Jonathan Swift
    d. In (b) and (c), but not in (a)

23. *Twenty-Six Men and a Girl* by Maxim Gorky, *A Rose for Emily* by William Faulkner, *I, Robot* by Isaac Asimov, and *The Virgin Suicides* by Jeffrey Eugenides all share which narrative point of view?

    a. Third-person singular
    b. First-person plural
    c. First-person singular
    d. Third-person plural

24. In which of these types of narrative voices does the narrator know everything about a particular character, including what s/he thinks and feels, but cannot speak about anything not known to that character?

    a. Third-person omniscient objective
    b. Third-person limited objective
    c. Third-person limited subjective
    d. Third-person omniscient subjective

25. Of these literary works that all use alternating-person narrative voices in the same book, which one(s) do(es) so with each viewpoint corresponding to a different chapter?
   a. Erin Hunter's *Warriors, Seekers,* and *Survivors* series
   b. The *Harry Potter* series of novels by J. K. Rowling
   c. *A Song of Ice and Fire* by George R. R. Martin
   d. Options (a) and (c) do this; (b) alternates differently

26. According to Aristotle's *Poetics,* which of these is necessary to a tragedy's plot?
   a. *Deus ex machina*
   b. Episodic events
   c. Unity of action
   d. External links

27. In the *Poetics,* Aristotle defined necessary components of tragic plot structure, including how some relate to cause and effect. Which of the following did he write about these?
   a. Exposition emphasizes effects over causes.
   b. Rising action emphasizes causes, not effects.
   c. Outcome emphasizes causes, not effects.
   d. Dénouement emphasizes effect, not causes.

28. As related to literary plot, which statement about conflict is most accurate?
   a. Characters' endeavors to resolve conflicts drive forward plot movement.
   b. Resolving a conflict(s) is often the primary endeavor for the protagonist.
   c. Emotional, mental, and/or moral conflicts add excitement and suspense.
   d. Many readers can find physical conflicts to be more personally satisfying.

29. Which choice gives the most accurate differential definitions of mood and tone in literature?
   a. Mood and tone are both synonyms referring to the emotional atmosphere of the work.
   b. Mood is the emotion evoked in the reader by the work; tone is the author's emotion.
   c. Mood is the emotion expressed by a work's author; tone is reader emotion it evokes.
   d. Mood is established by authors using different literary techniques than in creating tone.

30. Regarding story events in literary fiction, what is many authors' experience?
   a. Story events help readers understand event causality instead of motives.
   b. Story events are mental experiments that enable exploration for readers.
   c. Story events most often define a specific meaning in life or a way of living.
   d. Story events can explain motives and causes yet nothing of life's meaning.

31. Which of the following should authors of literary fiction AVOID when writing dialogue?
   a. Use dialogue to copy real conversations verbatim
   b. Use dialogue for more than breaking up narrative
   c. Use dialogue to supply exposition but be credible
   d. Use dialogue making it dynamic rather than static

32. In "The Story of an Hour" by Kate Chopin (1894), in which of these does the author use the plot structure element of discourse, including sequence and selection, to augment reader surprise at the story's outcome?

    a. Narrating some events out of their chronological order
    b. Omitting some details, like Brently Mallard's trip home
    c. Omitting all description of Louise, letting actions speak
    d. Options (a) and (b), but not (c)

33. Of the following, which describes what readers can do to analyze literary character development?

    a. Determining whether a character is dynamic or static is irrelevant to analyze character development
    b. Determining whether a character is "flat" or "round" is immaterial to analyze character development
    c. Determining whether a character symbolizes universal qualities cannot aid in analyzing development
    d. Determining whether characters' traits can be compared or contrasted helps analysis of development

34. In his poem "The Eagle," Alfred Tennyson includes this verse: "He clasps the crag with crooked hands." This incorporates which types of figurative language? Select all choices that apply.

    a. Simile
    b. Imagery
    c. Metaphor
    d. Alliteration
    e. Personification

35. In his poem "As I Walked Out One Evening" (1940), W. H. Auden writes, "I'll love you, dear, I'll love you/Till China and Africa meet, /And the river jumps over the mountain/And the salmon sing in the street." This stanza uses an example of which type of literary device/figurative language?

    a. Hubris
    b. Hyperbole
    c. Hyperbaton
    d. (a) and (c) only

36. In his epic poem *The Song of Hiawatha* (1855), how does Henry Wadsworth Longfellow most use poetic devices?

    a. He uses couplets to answer questions asked before.
    b. He uses couplets to clarify development of a theme.
    c. He uses meter that evokes the rhythms of chanting.
    d. He uses irony to help in development of the theme.

37. Which of the following reading strategies can teachers help students use as literacy skills to support active reading *before*, *during*, and *after* they read?

    a. Predicting what will occur in a text
    b. Summarizing the content of a text
    c. Identifying text-to-self connection
    d. (b) and (c), but only two of three with (a)

38. For evaluating a student's summary of a passage from literature, what is a valid criterion?

    a. The summary should be concise, even at the expense of completeness.
    b. The summary should include the reactions and opinions the reader had.
    c. The summary should cover points in proportion to the reader's interest.
    d. The summary should tag attributions, cite sources, and limit quotations.

39. Which statement most accurately represents how evidence-based instructional approaches should be evaluated for effectiveness?

    a. Assessors define what teaching practices are used during the evaluation.
    b. Ongoing monitoring is unnecessary as the evaluation identifies practices.
    c. Appropriate, established measures are used to evaluate student results.
    d. Student progress can be assessed without comparing teaching methods.

40. Regarding research-based teaching strategies that help students use the metacognitive process, which of these is most accurate?

    a. Whether an author gives a distorted or accurate view of reality aids self-monitoring
    b. Whether and to whom they would recommend the text is irrelevant to connecting
    c. Whether a text title is or is not interesting to them should not influence their reading
    d. Whether a text is effective on its audience is less important than techniques used

41. Which of the following analogies or statements is correct about language in informational text?

    a. Literal language is to denotation as figurative language is to connotation.
    b. Literal language is to connotation as figurative language is to denotation.
    c. It would be incorrect to make any analogy with any of these four terms.
    d. Informational text only uses literal language and only word denotations.

42. Of the following phrases often found in informational texts, which use language for figurative meanings? Select all choices that apply.

    a. A mountain of evidence
    b. A plethora of evidence
    c. A flood of responses
    d. A cascade of events
    e. A series of events

43. What is most accurate about reading comprehension of informational text?

    a. Comprehension of informational text depends only on retrieving important information.
    b. Comprehension of informational text depends only on inferences based on information.
    c. Comprehension of informational text depends on inference and recalling information.
    d. Comprehension of informational text includes inference but not prior reader knowledge.

44. If an individual is reading a nonfiction expository or informational text, which of the following inferences would the reader most appropriately make?

- a. Inferences regarding causes and effects
- b. Inferences about problems and solutions
- c. Inferences on a message the author sends
- d. Inferences about (a) and (b) more than (c)

45. What is a standard skill for students in grades 6-12 as it pertains to reading informational texts?

- a. Identifying textual evidence, but not its comparative strength or weakness
- b. Citing textual evidence supporting inferences and analyses, not conclusions
- c. Citing textual evidence that is strong and also citing evidence that is thorough
- d. Identifying things that are clear in an informational text but not unclear things

46. When students read informational text, they must be able to connect it with their existing knowledge and draw inferences from it to do which of the following?

- a. Comprehend the material enough to make conclusions, critical judgments, and interpretations
- b. Comprehend the material in the informational text thoroughly without doing anything further
- c. Comprehend the material and then make conclusions about it instead of any critical judgment
- d. Comprehend the material and produce their own interpretations of it rather than conclusions

47. When teachers assign students to use a paired reading strategy in an exercise to enhance comprehension through identifying main ideas and details in an informational text, what does this typically include?

- a. Reading aloud
- b. Silent reading
- c. (a) and (b)
- d. None of the above

48. Which of the following is an accurate statement about text coding (Harvey and Daniels, 2009) as an active reading strategy?

- a. Text coding refers to having students write computer code.
- b. Text coding is a strategy that some also call text monitoring.
- c. Text coding and text monitoring are two different strategies.
- d. Text coding can be done by students with no teacher model.

49. In the active reading strategy of text coding, which choice accurately represents what one of the codes used signifies?

- a. The code for "I know this" is a check mark.
- b. The code for "I know this" is an asterisk (*).
- c. The code for "I know this" is the letter "X."
- d. The code for "I know this" is an exclamation point (!).

50. In the two-column notes active reading strategy, using Lincoln's Gettysburg Address as an example, which of the following clauses or phrases would go under the column of main ideas?

    a. "Four score and seven years ago"
    b. "Our fathers brought forth... a new nation"
    c. "Conceived in Liberty"
    d. "Dedicated to the proposition that all men are created equal."

51. Among the following techniques whereby authors of informational text connect and distinguish ideas, which one is capable of showing both similarities *and* differences?

    a. Comparing
    b. Analogizing
    c. Contrasting
    d. Categorizing

52. Which of the following statements is/are true about a glossary and an index in an informational text? Select all choices that apply.

    a. Only one is in alphabetical order.
    b. Only one is in the back of a book.
    c. Only one lists a book's main topics.
    d. Only one lists entries' page numbers.
    e. Only one provides definitions of terms.

53. Which of the following sentences uses the word *smart* for a connotative rather than denotative meaning?

    a. Asked where his homework was, he gave a smart retort.
    b. Sandy got detention for having a smart mouth all period.
    c. Wendell was smart to arrive early on the day of the test.
    d. (a) and (b) use the connotation, but (c) uses denotation.

54. How should technical language used in a scientific informational text differ from vernacular (everyday) or literary language used in other texts? Select all choices that apply.

    a. It should be more grandiose.
    b. It should be more impersonal.
    c. It should be more professional.
    d. It should be more self-deprecating.
    e. It should always be in passive voice.

55. Kate Chopin begins her short story "Regret" by describing the main character as having "a good strong figure, ruddy cheeks, hair that was changing from brown to gray, and a determined eye." What is an example of implicit meaning in this sentence? Select all choices that apply.

    a. She was no longer young.
    b. She had a solid physique.
    c. She had good circulation.
    d. She looked determined.
    e. She had determination.

56. Which of the following is true about the author's point of view or purpose in an informational text?

a. Readers can always identify this because informational authors state it explicitly.
b. Readers will have to infer this when an informational author never identifies it.
c. Readers can identify it equally from neutral, balanced, or opinionated positions.
d. Readers who have to analyze text to identify this can assume it is poorly written.

57. If an author of informational text makes a reference to someone famous, e.g., the name of a literary or historical figure, to create resonance with readers and/or make something or someone in the text symbolic, what rhetorical device is this?

a. Allusion
b. Paradox
c. Analogy
d. Parody

58. Among persuasive methods of appeal, which of the following writing techniques supports the author's views by quoting others who agree with them?

a. Anticipating objections
b. Citing expert opinions
c. Bandwagon appeals
d. Testimonials

59. Which statement is correct as a criterion for critically evaluating the effectiveness of an informational text author's methods of appeal to readers?

a. The author's thesis matters, but why s/he chose it does not.
b. An author should offer realistic solutions to problems raised.
c. Offering problem solutions is key, regardless of their realism.
d. The thesis and central ideas supersede supporting evidence.

60. Reasons that authors of technical informational text may need to write in non-technical language include which of the following?

a. To communicate denser content rather than messages
b. To inform one's colleagues who work in the same field
c. To procure economic support for budgets and projects
d. To inform a narrow range of citizens having knowledge

61. What most accurately represents some of the steps to take and their sequence for readers to evaluate arguments in informational text?

a. Readers should identify premises supporting an argument's conclusion first, and then the conclusion.
b. Readers should identify an argument's conclusion first, and then identify the premises supporting it.
c. Readers should list an argument's conclusion and supporting premises in their order of identification.
d. Readers should try to paraphrase premises to clarify them, not to make them fit with the conclusion.

62. Which statement is most accurate about reader identification of author purpose in informational writing?

a. Considering why an author wrote a text affords greater insights to it
b. Considering why an author wrote a text inhibits critical reading skills
c. Considering why an author wrote a text inhibits reader expectations
d. Considering why an author wrote a text allows less reader response

63. Among logical fallacies in rhetoric, what does the term *post hoc ergo propter hoc* mean?

a. It is Latin for "What follows is irrelevant distraction."
b. It is Latin for "This does not follow," a non sequitur.
c. It is Latin for "After this, therefore because of this."
d. It is Latin for "This parody of an actual claim is false."

64. For educated consumers to critically evaluate multiple information sources in various media, which of these accurately represents things they should consider?

a. Who is delivering the message matters more than the reason.
b. Methods for capturing and sustaining attention are irrelevant.
c. The type of medium supersedes the point of view expressed.
d. Alternative potential interpretations inform critical evaluation.

65. To evaluate books and articles as specific media sources, what is valid about criteria to use?

a. Any historical perspectives are irrelevant for judging books.
b. Consider if journals contain advertising and, if so, for what.
c. For evaluating books, currency of information is immaterial.
d. Author biographies and book reviews cannot inform a user.

66. Which of these most accurately represents persuasive techniques used in various media for advertising?

a. Persuasion via humor is used more often in news and advocacy than in advertising.
b. Qualifiers, better known as "weasel words," typically accompany understatement.
c. Hyperbole (exaggeration), superlatives, and other intensifiers are least persuasive.
d. Repetition and appeals to audience sentiment are both effective persuasive tools.

67. Among the following, what defines an adverb as a part of speech?

a. It serves to name a person, place, or thing
b. It serves to name an action or state of being
c. It modifies a verb, adjective, or another adverb
d. It modifies or describes a noun or adjective

68. "I would like to go with you; however, I won't have time." In this sentence, what part of speech is the word "however?"

a. Preposition
b. Conjunction
c. Conjunctive adverb
d. Subordinating conjunction

69. **"The teacher explained the answers to the students who ask questions." Which of the following corrects any error in this sentence?**
   a. "The teacher explains"
   b. "the students who asked"
   c. Either (a) or (b), not both
   d. There is no error in the sentence.

70. **Identify the grammatical error in the following sentence:**

   Children who hug seldom are shy.
   a. Lack of parallelism
   b. Split infinitive
   c. Squinting modifier
   d. Subject-verb disagreement

71. **Identify the grammatical error in the following sentence:**

   They liked to stay at home, cook dinner, and watching TV.
   a. Lack of parallelism
   b. Split infinitive
   c. Squinting modifier
   d. Subject-verb disagreement

72. **Identify the grammatical error in the following sentence:**

   There is a lot of people outside complaining.
   a. Lack of parallelism
   b. Split infinitive
   c. Squinting modifier
   d. Subject-verb disagreement

73. **Identify the grammatical error in the following sentence:**

   There is no reason to loudly shout your answers.
   a. Lack of parallelism
   b. Split infinitive
   c. Squinting modifier
   d. Subject-verb disagreement

74. **Which of the following versions of this sentence is punctuated correctly?**
   a. Not all permission slips were returned, moreover the bus was unavailable.
   b. Not all permission slips were returned; moreover, the bus was unavailable.
   c. Not all permission slips were returned, moreover; the bus was unavailable.
   d. Not all permission slips were returned, moreover, the bus was unavailable.

75. **Mechanically, which of the following sentences is correct?**
   a. Those gloves are her's, but the Browns say that book is their's.
   b. Those gloves are hers, but the Brown's say that book is theirs.
   c. Those gloves are her's, but the Brown's say that book is their's.
   d. Those gloves are hers, but the Browns say that book is theirs.

12

76. "We will depart as a class, but when we arrive we will split up into small groups." In this sentence, which part(s) is/are (a) prepositional phrase(s)?

    a. "as a class"
    b. "when we arrive"
    c. "into small groups"
    d. (a) and (c) but not (b)

77. "Although Ted had an impressive education, he had little experience working with individuals, which made him less effective at relating to them." Which kinds of clauses does this sentence contain?

    a. Two dependent clauses and one independent clause
    b. One dependent clause and two independent clauses
    c. Two independent clauses and no dependent clauses
    d. One dependent clause and one independent clause

78. "Every time they visited, she got to know him a little bit better." Which structure does this sentence have?

    a. Simple
    b. Complex
    c. Compound
    d. Compound-complex

79. "The tall man wearing a black raincoat, a yellow hat, and one red shoe entered the restaurant, walked to the back, and sat down alone at the smallest table farthest away from the staff and other patrons." This sentence has which of the following structures?

    a. Simple
    b. Complex
    c. Compound
    d. Compound-complex

80. Which of the following suffixes is NOT commonly used to form a noun from some other part of speech?

    a. -ation
    b. -ness
    c. -ity
    d. -ize

81. Of these four types of context clues, which one involves antonyms?

    a. Definitions
    b. Describing
    c. Opposites
    d. Examples

82. Which of the following most accurately reflects what readers can determine about a word they do not know through the syntax of a sentence in text?

    a. Nearly always what the word's meaning is, and sometimes what part of speech the word is
    b. Sometimes the meaning of a word, and also nearly always what part of speech that word is
    c. Nearly always both what part of speech a word is, and also what the meaning of the word is
    d. Sometimes both what part of speech the word is and also what the meaning of the word is

83. Regarding nuances of meaning in written words, which of these is an example of conveying *subjective* connotations through the use of *diction*?
   a. Describing the engine of a car using the adjective "greasy"
   b. Describing someone's hair and smile with the adjective "greasy"
   c. Describing clothes via lyrics "Don we now our gay apparel"
   d. Describing same-sex preferences and homosexuality as "gay"

84. Which of the following reference sources would help a reader find out the meaning of a specialized vocabulary or terminology word in a technical or subject-specific text?
   a. Glossary
   b. Dictionary
   c. Style manual
   d. Spell checker

85. Of the following attributes of a literary character, which do authors portray by using diction rather than dialect?
   a. Social class
   b. Geographic region
   c. Cultural background
   d. Individual characteristics

86. Author Frances O'Roark Dowell used a late 1920s Appalachian Mountain regional dialect in her award-winning novel *Dovey Coe* (2000) for the narration. Why might she have done this?
   a. Because the author is most comfortable speaking in this dialect
   b. Because this dialect was natural to the setting and the narrator
   c. Because the unusual language would attract readers' attention
   d. Because it contrasted with the characters, establishing tension

87. The research-based approach to language teaching and learning called Styles- and Strategies-Based Instruction (SSBI) consists of five phases. Which of the following arranges these phases in the correct order of instruction?
   a. Strategy Preparation, Strategy Awareness-Raising, Strategy Training, Strategy Practice, Strategy Personalization
   b. Strategy Awareness-Raising, Strategy Preparation, Strategy Practice, Strategy Personalization, Strategy Training
   c. Strategy Training, Strategy Practice, Strategy Preparation, Strategy Personalization, Strategy Awareness-Raising
   d. Strategy Personalization, Strategy Awareness-Raising, Strategy Preparation, Strategy Training, Strategy Practice

88. According to research into vocabulary instruction methods, which of the following aspects is NOT identified as requiring further investigation?
   a. Receptive vocabulary vs. productive vocabulary
   b. Written and print vocabulary vs. spoken vocabulary
   c. Vocabulary definitions vs. vocabulary contexts
   d. Depth of vocabulary vs. breadth of vocabulary

14

89. Studies evaluating instructional methods for language acquisition and vocabulary development have found which of the following?
   a. Adding multimedia applications reduces learning gaps between ELL and other students.
   b. Adding multimedia applications enhances learning equally for ELL and all other students.
   c. Children have more difficulty recalling meanings of new words than their pronunciations.
   d. Adding teacher questions and comments interferes with acquiring new word meanings.

90. Which of the following is a primary function of argumentative writing?
   a. To introduce readers to some new information
   b. To explain how a process functions to readers
   c. To develop an idea or concept for the readers
   d. To prove a point that will convince the readers

91. Among skills that students need to learn for writing informative or explanatory text, which one involves *only* text-to-self connections?
   a. Locating and selecting topic-related primary and secondary sources
   b. Combining information about the topic with existing knowledge
   c. Developing writing skills with making comparisons and contrasts
   d. Developing writing skills to create transitions and cite examples

92. Which statement is most accurate regarding journals as a form of writing?
   a. Journals are only for confiding and processing personal experiences in private.
   b. Journals need never be edited for mechanics because nobody will ever see them.
   c. Journals may be expected or hoped by some authors to be published one day.
   d. Journals may be shared with readers, but are never therapeutic for an author.

93. Of the following, which is true about both *The Diary of a Young Girl* by Anne Frank (1947) and *Go Ask Alice* by Beatrice Sparks (1971), in addition to the fact that both are written in diary form?
   a. They both are the diaries of 20th-century teenage girls.
   b. They both are fictional novels created by the authors.
   c. They both communicate negative perspectives on life.
   d. They both end with the survival of the main character.

94. Which of these is a correct statement about the epistolary genre of writing?
   a. The New Testament Epistles of Apostles to Christians are the only true examples of this.
   b. In modern literature, epistolary novels were most popular in the 18th and 19th centuries.
   c. The epistolary genre developed a long time after the ancient Egyptian civilization ended.
   d. In epistolary novels, the story is typically told in third person by the omniscient narrator.

95. The introduction of an essay should answer three questions. Which of those answers represents the writer's thesis statement?
   a. What the subject of the essay will be
   b. How the essay addresses the subject
   c. How the author structured this essay
   d. What this essay is supposed to prove

96. When writing an essay, which is the best way to address multiple main points?

    a. Cover all main points, supporting evidence, and its relation to thesis in a single long paragraph.

    b. Introduce each point in one paragraph, support it in another, and relate it to the thesis in another.

    c. Cover each point, the evidence supporting it, and its relation to the thesis in a separate paragraph.

    d. How the writer addresses multiple main points in an essay is completely individual preference.

97. Regarding essay writing, which of these is accurate about the organization of essays?

    a. Well-organized essays are more likely to gain readers' acceptance of their theses as valid.

    b. Well-organized essays have better structure but are less likely to hold readers' attention.

    c. Well-organized essays are easier for writers to compose yet harder for readers to follow.

    d. Well-organized essays give readers better guides, but are harder for writers to compose.

98. Which of these is/are most applicable to differences of online blogs vs. print articles?

    a. Blogs are not expected by readers to be as high in quality as print.

    b. Blogs must be more legible and use more predictive text features.

    c. Blogs afford less complexity to format and write than newspapers.

    d. Blogs can be skimmed by readers the same way as printed articles.

99. Which mode of writing is most suitable for the purpose of encouraging the reading audience to explore ideas and consider various potential associated responses?

    a. Narrative

    b. Expository

    c. Persuasive

    d. Speculative

100. Among the following, which is the best example of writing for certain purposes?

    a. An older student writes in simpler vocabulary, syntax, and printing for younger readers.

    b. A writer's word choice and diction stimulate readers' feelings of empathy and sympathy.

    c. A writer's word choice and diction stimulate readers to challenge opposing viewpoints.

    d. Writers select different (expository, persuasive, narrative, etc.) formats and language.

101. What is an example of how students can write most appropriately for different tasks, purposes, and audiences?

    a. Using sophisticated language writing for their classmates

    b. Using simple language to request privileges from their parents

    c. Using vivid, entertaining language with younger students

    d. Using humor to ask parent permission for independent activity

102. In an analogy comparing an essay, article, or paper to a table, how should parts of the table represent parts of the written composition?

    a. Each leg is a main idea while the top is all of the supporting evidence.

    b. The top is the main idea and each leg is a group of supporting details.

    c. Each leg is one paragraph and the top of the table is the central idea.

    d. The top is the introductory paragraph and the legs are all the others.

Mometrix

103. Suppose a student writes, "My dog is not very bright" as a main point in a composition. Which of the following is an example of additional information that supports this point?

   a. "Every time I leave the house to go to school, he cries."
   b. "When I come home every day, he is always happy to see me."
   c. "At the age of 5 years, he still does not answer to his name."
   d. "He loves to play fetch and will not tire of the game for hours."

104. Which of these is characteristic of poor focus making a written paragraph ineffective?

   a. A paragraph having unrelated sentences
   b. A paragraph having one or too few ideas
   c. A paragraph having ideas with transitions
   d. A paragraph having excess generalization

105. Among the following structural patterns in a paragraph, which does a writer use to show readers something instead of telling them something?

   a. Division
   b. Narration
   c. Definition
   d. Description

106. Which of the following is most characteristic of paragraph coherence in writing?

   a. The parts of the paragraph are clearly and discretely separated.
   b. The parts of the paragraph flow well from one part to the next.
   c. Conceptual content is given using contrasting structural patterns.
   d. Control at the sentence level undermines paragraph coherence.

107. A cohesive written paragraph is described by all EXCEPT which of these characteristics?

   a. Its sentences are unified by ideas that fit together.
   b. Its sentences flow easily from one to the next.
   c. Its sentences connect from old to new information.
   d. Its sentences start with old material and end with new material.

108. Which of these is a fact regarding cohesion and coherence in paragraph writing?

   a. A paragraph can be cohesive but not coherent, not the reverse.
   b. A paragraph can be coherent but not cohesive, not the reverse.
   c. A paragraph can be cohesive but not coherent, or it can be the reverse.
   d. A paragraph that is cohesive is always coherent and also the reverse.

109. To compose cohesive and coherent paragraphs, which of the following should writers do?

   a. Begin sentences by introducing new information
   b. Introduce sentences with long, complex clauses
   c. Make the transitions between ideas transparent
   d. Vary and alternate topics addressed throughout

17

110. In composing an essay or similar piece, in which sequence should a writer do the following?
   a. List all details supporting each main point, organize details in sequential order, narrow topics to a main idea, find which main points support the main idea, decide how to sequence main points
   b. Decide how to sequence main points, narrow topics to a main idea, find which main points support the main idea, organize details in sequential order, list all details supporting each main point
   c. Organize details in sequential order, decide how to sequence main points, list all details supporting each main point, narrow topics to a main idea, find which main points support the main idea
   d. Narrow topics to a main idea, find which main points support the main idea, decide how to sequence main points, list all details supporting each main point, organize details in sequential order

111. Regarding the strength and closure that a written composition's conclusion should have, which of these indicates a conclusion that does NOT achieve closure?
   a. Readers perceive from the conclusion that the main points made were meaningful and important.
   b. Readers perceive from the conclusion that the writer said what was needed, so the work is complete.
   c. Readers perceive from the conclusion that the writer reached the required word count and stopped.
   d. Readers perceive from the conclusion that evidence supporting main points was well-developed.

112. When a researcher writes a paper to report on a study, which functions does the statement of the research question or problem serve?
   a. Identifies the issue but not why the researcher cares about it
   b. Identifies the variables of focus rather than why they matter
   c. Identifies the issue, its importance, and the scope of research
   d. Identifies only scope of research and variables of study focus

113. To evaluate the credibility of research sources, which of the following is a valid consideration?
   a. It is credible if published in a peer-reviewed scholarly journal.
   b. It is never credible if it is a source which was published online.
   c. It is not found to be more credible through author affiliations.
   d. It is immaterial to credibility how many times a source is cited.

114. Which statement is accurate regarding guidelines for searching when conducting a review of the literature for writing a research paper?
   a. Too many references indicate the research question is not narrow enough.
   b. Too few references indicate the area of investigation is not specific enough.
   c. No references at all indicate the topic and research question must be invalid.
   d. Researchers should not plan their searches as they will find more references.

115. Of the following source types you may cite in a research paper, which one requires the largest number of citation components?

    a. A book that is printed on paper
    b. A book that is published online
    c. A journal article printed on paper
    d. A journal article published online

116. Regarding major style manuals, for students citing references in research papers, which of these is most accurate?

    a. Which style manual to use is always obvious by subject.
    b. If not stated in the syllabus, students should always ask.
    c. The professor or instructor always has one preferred style.
    d. For citations it does not matter because all styles are the same.

117. Which statement is most appropriate regarding how students should integrate quotations from research sources into their papers?

    a. Summarize each source quoted before continuing an argument
    b. When quoting sources, longer quotations give greater authority
    c. Parenthetical quotations within sentences make integration seamless
    d. Students can use fewer words than a quotation to respond to it

118. Among these components of speech delivery, which is most effective for establishing rapport and personal connection with audiences?

    a. Eye contact
    b. Vocal tones
    c. Articulation
    d. Movement

119. What is accurate about factors influencing choices among media for communicating ideas?

    a. The budget available to the presenter is the sole influence.
    b. When using mass media, a target audience is not relevant.
    c. For social change, potential audience participation matters.
    d. The duration of a message has no effect on media choices.

120. In evaluating whether information is presented concisely in a speech, which of the following criteria applies?

    a. Making a point or answering a question takes five minutes to keep audience attention.
    b. If a speaker includes too many details or anecdotes, an audience will become confused.
    c. Speakers should incorporate equal amounts of necessary and interesting information.
    d. Speakers should avoid pausing before answering questions so they appear prepared.

121. In digital media, which of these advantages for diverse students can be accomplished, including automatically, through cross-media transformations?

    a. Students can underline all summary sentences in detailed texts.
    b. Teachers can italicize all words in a text with Greek or Latin roots.
    c. Students can boldface new or unfamiliar vocabulary words in a text.
    d. Teachers and students can convert speech to text and text to speech.

122. Among technology-based strategies for enhancing understanding of communication goals, which of the following is an advantage of web media?
   a. They give global information access
   b. They need designers and managers
   c. They must have content contributors
   d. They entail accessing technical support

123. Which of these accurately reflects a research-based strategy for writing instruction?
   a. Brainstorming is a technique too open-ended for students planning writing.
   b. Giving students steps to follow for argumentative writing is too structured.
   c. Explicit instruction in planning, revision, and editing improves performance.
   d. Collaborative writing deprives students of independently practicing writing.

124. Among these procedural devices that help students plan and revise writing, which one is for helping them remember key sets of information?
   a. Mnemonic devices
   b. Graphic organizers
   c. Making outlines
   d. Using checklists

125. Of the following statements, which correctly describes research findings about effective writing instruction techniques?
   a. Exposing students to the processes of writing is sufficient.
   b. Teacher modeling and think-alouds are deemed effective.
   c. Providing students with scaffolding is an unneeded crutch.
   d. Implicit and embedded instruction is better than explicit instruction.

126. Which of these is a correct statement about how to use a rubric relative to writing instruction and/or assessment?
   a. Students should use a rubric as a guide in what and how to write.
   b. The teacher should not explain the rubric to students in advance.
   c. Rubrics are for teachers to use in assessment and not otherwise.
   d. Teachers should only use rubrics for organizing their lesson plans.

127. How can teachers use portfolio assessments to evaluate student writing?
   a. As formative assessments
   b. As summative assessments
   c. As both kinds of assessments
   d. As neither kind of assessment

128. Teachers must consider student developmental levels when assigning cooperative learning projects and/or discussions. For example, students are bored by topics at younger age levels and lost by topics at older ones. In addition to chronological age, which other developmental level does this example relate to most?
   a. Social developmental levels
   b. Cognitive developmental levels
   c. Emotional developmental levels
   d. Behavioral developmental levels

129. Regarding how educators can address cultural diversity in the classroom, which of these statements is true?

    a. Cultural differences influence the beliefs of students instead of their behaviors.
    b. Individual differences in students supersede all cultural differences in students.
    c. Disabilities in students supersede all individual and cultural student differences.
    d. Teachers who acknowledge student cultural differences avert student isolation.

130. Which statement is correct regarding communication skills that teachers need to build relationships with diverse students, parents, and families?

    a. It is more important to disagree respectfully than recognize cultural differences.
    b. It is more important to respect confidentiality than to be willing to compromise.
    c. It is more important to communicate responsibly than to prove that one is right.
    d. It is more important to tolerate others' perspectives than listening to them closely.

131. Of the following, which reflect(s) elements of creating safe educational environments where students can learn to read, write, listen, and speak? Select all choices that apply.

    a. Teachers must create student-teacher relationships having reciprocal trust.
    b. Teachers must gain students' trust, but they need not also trust students.
    c. Teachers must let students know they only care about them academically.
    d. Teachers must let students know they only care about them personally.
    e. Teachers must let students know they care academically and personally.

Answer Key and Explanations

1. B: O. Henry wrote a novel, *Cabbages and Kings,* as well as many short stories. Herman Melville (c) and Nathaniel Hawthorne wrote both novels and short stories. All three were 19th-century American authors. However, Charles Dickens (b), who also wrote novels and short stories, was a 19th-century British author.

2. D: *Beowulf* is an epic poem by an anonymous poet written in Old English (c. 700-1000). The Odyssey (b) is an epic poem orally composed by Homer in ancient Greek (c. 760-700 BC). The Divine Comedy (c) is an epic poem written by Dante Alighieri in Tuscan Italian (1320). *The Decameron* (d) is a series of novellas within a frame tale (like Geoffrey Chaucer's *Canterbury Tales,* which it influenced) rather than an epic poem, written by Giovanni Boccaccio in Florentine Italian (1353).

3. A: William Shakespeare published *Hamlet* in 1601 in England; Jamestown, the first American colony, was established in Virginia in 1607. Columbus first visited the Americas in 1492; Chaucer, who wrote *The Canterbury Tales* in England, died in 1400 (b). Following Parliament's 11-year reign (the Commonwealth Period), Charles II was restored to the English throne in 1660, beginning the Restoration; John Milton published *Paradise Lost* in 1667 (c). Irish author James Joyce published *Finnegans Wake* in 1939 and American author Richard Wright published *Native Son* in 1940, both before World War II ended (d) in 1945.

4. C: Louisa May Alcott published *Little Women* in 1868 and sets the novel during the Civil War. Mark Twain published *The Adventures of Tom Sawyer* (a) in 1876, inspired by his own childhood and containing liberal amounts of satire and humor, likely set in the mid-1840s and not reflecting the Civil War. Harriet Beecher Stowe published *Uncle Tom's Cabin* (b) in 1852, before the war, in reaction to the 1850 Fugitive Slave Act and with the purpose of promoting abolition with Northern readers. Historians often view her novel as instrumental in the Civil War's onset. Herman Melville published *Moby-Dick* (d), which includes slavery among its themes, in 1851, also before the war.

5. B: The division described in the question is termed a stanza in poetry. A verse (a) is the term for a single line rather than a group of lines in poetry. (In ballads and songs it can mean a group of lines as a stanza does in poems.) A refrain (c) is a line(s), verse(s), or other set of the same or similar words that is/are repeated regularly throughout a ballad, other poem, or song, often alternating with verses. A paragraph (d) is the term for the analogous division, in *prose* only.

6. A: This describes the form and purpose of haiku, originating in Japanese poetic tradition, adopted and adapted for other languages. (Japanese haiku can be translated for meaning, but doing so alters the number of syllables.) American poet Ezra Pound reproduced haiku's intent and syllabication* in his 1911 poem "In a Station of the Metro": "The apparition of these faces in the crowd; /Petals on a wet, black bough." Ballads (b), sonnets (c), and limericks (d) do not follow this structure or function. *(Though not printed as such, line 1=5/7. Pound's two lines nearly rhyme; Japanese haiku typically do not.)

7. D: Epigrams are rhyming couplets (two lines) or single lines of poetry designed to be memorable by their cleverness, word choice, and brevity. An example is Benjamin Franklin's "Early to bed and early to rise/Makes a man healthy, wealthy, and wise." Odes (a), very popular during the Romantic period, are poems conveying emotional and/or contemplative content. Epics (b) are long poems telling of adventures and heroic accomplishments. Elegies (c) are poems that mourn and memorialize the dead.

22

8. C: The novel of manners is characterized by language using impersonal, standardized formulas (a); inhibited emotional expression (b); symbolic representation of some secure, established social order (c); and descriptions of whichever society it involves, including its defined codes of behavior (d). Some of the best examples of novels of manners are those by Jane Austen (e.g., *Sense and Sensibility, Pride and Prejudice, Mansfield Park, Emma, Northanger Abbey, Persuasion,* etc.).

9. A: *Bildungsromans* are novels of formation, education, and culture, depicting their main characters' processes of searching, learning, and coming of age. Johann Wolfgang von Goethe's *Wilhelm Meister's Apprenticeship* (1796) is widely considered the original *Bildungsroman*. Goethe's (1774) novel *The Sorrows of Young Werther* (b), however, is an epistolary (written in the form of correspondence or letters) tragic romantic novel that is not considered a *Bildungsroman*. Charles Dickens' 1850 novel *David Copperfield* (d) and 1861 novel *Great Expectations* (c) are also examples of this genre, but not considered the first.

10. B: Realistic authors strive to represent reality as closely as possible, even in fiction: they avoid exaggeration, which satire often employs to ridicule social behaviors. Both genres may be written in a serious tone (a) compatible with realism but also useful in satire: Jonathan Swift intensifies the satirical effects of *A Modest Proposal* by making absurd and even horrific recommendations in an ostensibly serious tone. Realists may depict situational irony, e.g., O. Henry in "The Gift of the Magi"; irony is a key satirists' tool. Writing dialogue in the vernacular (d) is a realistic technique equally appropriate in satire.

11. D: Choice (a) uses only literal meaning by describing the willow's appearance factually: it has branches that are long and that trail. Choice (b) uses figurative meaning with a simile that explicitly compares the willow's leaves to teardrops in appearance. Choice (c) also uses figurative language with a metaphor that implies comparison by describing the willow as weeping into the stream, as well as anthropomorphism by giving human qualities to the non-human willow.

12. B: The author wanted readers to infer the main character/narrator is indeed quite mad—not only because he repeatedly and strenuously denies he is, but moreover because he irrationally believes his calculating, careful planning, deception, and pretense of kindness are proof of his sanity *in planning a murder*—and his calmness in telling the story is further "proof" of his "sanity." If option (a) were true, then option (c) could logically follow, but option (b) would be false (d). However, the reverse is true, so options (a), (c), and (d) are all incorrect.

13. C: Charles Dickens used a series of opposites to convey the idea that the period described involved conflicts between extremes of positive and negative, matched so equally that neither could win. He also introduced the tension of such conflicts around which the novel revolves—of love vs. hate and family vs. oppression. He was not ascribing all the contrasts to personal subjectivity (a), saying in comparing the past and present that they could not be separated (b), or attributing the extremes to the imagination of its most vocal experts (d).

14. D: The even rhythm, plus ample use of anaphora—repeating the same phrase starting contiguous clauses ("it was the age... it was the age... it was the epoch... it was the epoch... it was the season... it was the season... we had... we had... we were all... we were all...")—introduce and emphasize the concept of equal, opposing forces; AND all the opposites introduce a pivotal "doubles" motif and structure—Sydney Carton and Charles Darnay, London and Paris, Miss Pross and Mme. Defarge, etc. This introduction uses anaphora, NOT anastrophe (c), which reverses adjective-noun order to noun-adjective (e.g., "ocean blue," "time immemorial," "trials unending," etc.).

15. C: In the sense that Charles Dickens uses them here, light and darkness do not literally mean physical illumination or its absence, but figuratively symbolize good and evil, knowledge and ignorance, happiness and unhappiness, hope and despair, etc. The other three choices all represent the use of words chosen for their literal meanings.

16. A: Because of the balancing of opposites in the introduction, readers can infer that the story may more likely achieve a similar balance than that it will present a greater proportion of either one (b), (c). Therefore, choice (d) is incorrect in that readers can infer nothing the story may include after the introduction.

17. B: Throughout history, teenagers have fallen in love; moreover, in Shakespeare's time when people did not live as long as today, serious love in adolescence was not necessarily even age-inappropriate. Thus Shakespeare does not attribute the tragedy to the characters' youth in this play (a). One theme in this play is the relationship of love and violence (c), with love often causing violence. Another theme is that of fate, which does control the characters (d) in this play, emphasized in the Chorus's first speech describing them as "star-crossed."

18. A: Victor Hugo shows how important love and compassion for others is in many ways. Receiving these transforms the main character, and his subsequent acts of love and compassion beget the same in others. Hugo also shows long-range impacts of the French Revolution on society, but not its success (b): though opposing the former monarchies and embracing the values inspiring the Revolution, he disagreed those values could be achieved with violence, showing this when describing the Battle of Waterloo. He also criticizes France's rigid class system, which persisted post-Revolution (c). Because choice (a) is correct, choice (d) is incorrect.

19. A: The narrator/main character never admits insanity. From the beginning he unequivocally denies it (b), simultaneously demonstrating it through his words and the deeds he relates. Edgar Allan Poe uses this denial to develop the theme: people who are completely crazy rarely admit or even realize it. He also develops the theme through the narrator's obsession with his victim's "evil eye" (c), which symbolizes the "I" and many other things, including the irrationality of the narrator's murderous impulse. The narrator's mistaking his own heartbeat for that of his dead victim (d) is Poe's ultimate thematic development.

20. A: God's destroying humans for their wickedness is a universal theme found in the book of Genesis, the Quran, and the Epic of Gilgamesh. In only two of three, God tells Noah in Genesis and Nuh in Gilgamesh to build a ship/ark to survive (b). Noah sends a dove and Utnapishtim a raven to test the flood's end (c); this is a shared story element, not a universal theme. The Quran tells of Allah destroying only people who deny or ignore his messages, and Genesis tells of God destroying everybody except Noah and family—again, these are story elements, not universal themes.

21. D: These characters share the universal theme of overreaching (representing excessive pride), overstepping one's boundaries, and going too far. In Genesis, Adam and Eve partook of the Tree of Knowledge; in Greek mythology, Prometheus shared knowledge of fire among humans; Icarus "went too far out" by flying too close to the sun, melting the wax cementing the wings his father Daedalus had made, so the wings fell apart and Icarus fell into the sea; in Ernest Hemingway's *The Old Man and the Sea,* fisherman Santiago in his boat, trying to catch the marlin, "went out too far."

22. D: In *Sherlock Holmes* (a), the first-person narrative is told by Dr. Watson, a close friend of main character Sherlock Holmes, but not the main character. In *The Tell-Tale Heart* (b) and *Gulliver's Travels* (c), the main characters are also the narrators, and they speak in the first person ("I," "me," etc.).

24

23. B: The first-person plural narrative voice is unusual in novels, but it can be effective as it is in the examples given in this question. This point of view uses "we," "us," and "our" rather than the first-person singular (c) "I," "me," and "my." Third-person singular (a) uses "he," "she," "it," "his," "her," "its," etc. Third-person plural (d) uses "they," "them," and "their," etc.

24. C: The third-person omniscient narrator knows everything about ALL characters, not just one particular one, but when the narration is objective (a), it does not include the characters' inner thoughts and feelings. The third-person limited narrator knows everything about one particular character, but does not tell that character's inner states in objective narration (b), whereas the third-person limited narrator may include one character's thoughts and feelings in subjective narration (c). The third-person omniscient subjective narrator (d) knows everything about all characters and includes their inner states in the narration.

25. D: Both Erin Hunter (a pseudonym for several authors) (a) and George R. R. Martin (c) alternate narrator points of view to correspond with new chapters in a book. However, while J. K. Rowling (b) also alternates narrative voices in her books among a third-person limited narrator and the voices of various characters (other than Harry Potter), she does not alternate them to correspond with new chapters.

26. C: Aristotle defined plot not as the story but as its structure. In his *Poetics,* he found that, for a tragedy's plot to be complete, it must have unity of action, meaning its events were not controlled by a *deus ex machina* (a) ("God out of a machine," i.e., some miraculous or magical resolution) or any other interventions from outside; and were linked internally, not externally (d) or episodic (b) in nature.

27. C: According to Aristotle, the exposition, also called the inciting moment, incentive, or simply the beginning, emphasizes causes over effects, not vice versa (a). The rising action, which he called *desis,* i.e., tying up, known today as the complication, features cause and effect equally (b). The dénouement, which Aristotle called *lusis,* or unraveling, and which followed the climax or turning point, also features cause and effect equally (d), but in more rapid succession than in the complication. The outcome or end emphasizes causes over effects (c).

28. A: One important aspect of how conflict relates to plot is that the characters' actions in pursuit of conflict resolution serve to drive the plot's forward movement. Resolving conflict is often the protagonist's most significant endeavor (b). While emotional, mental, and/or moral conflicts are often more personally satisfying to many readers (c), physical conflicts (e.g., wars, escapes, exploration, etc.) add excitement and suspense (d) to plots—not vice versa.

29. B: Mood refers to the emotions evoked in the reader by the literary work, whereas tone refers to the emotions and/or attitude of the author in writing it—not the reverse (c). Hence mood and tone do not mean the same thing (a). Though mood and tone have different meanings, authors establish both using the same literary techniques (d), e.g., vocabulary choices, descriptive writing, syntax, diction, figurative expressions, etc.

30. B: Many authors find story events can help readers understand both event causality and character motivation (a), as well as some of life's meaning (d). They describe story events as mental experiments that enable readers to explore (b) different meanings and ways of living. They say story events do NOT necessarily identify one specific or definitive meaning in life or prescribe one way of living for readers (c), but can define some meaning, shape, and direction in otherwise seemingly random events.

31. A: When composing literary fiction, writers should use dialogue effectively by NOT reproducing real-life conversations verbatim, but edit and rework it to omit boring and irrelevant parts. They SHOULD use dialogue for more than simply breaking up sections of narrative (b); to provide readers with needed exposition, yet maintain its credibility (c) as conversation; and make it dynamic rather than static (d) or similar to regular non-conversational prose.

32. D: Kate Chopin narrates some of the events in this story in a different order than they actually occur chronologically, and this makes the end more surprising to readers. She also omits some details. For example, there is no mention of Brently's trip home until he arrives, so readers are just as surprised as Louise is to see him (b). Chopin does NOT omit all description of Louise; she not only lets her actions speak (c) for her in many instances, but also uses description of her appearance and behavior to inform her character.

33. C: Some aspects of literary characters that readers can focus on to inform their analysis of authors' character development include: determining whether a character is dynamic, i.e., undergoes some significant change(s) in the story, or static, i.e., remains unchanged throughout (a); whether a character is "flat," i.e., not fully developed, or "round," i.e., well-developed with vividly salient personality traits (b); whether a character symbolizes any universal qualities (c); and whether they can compare and/or contrast one character's attributes to another's (d).

34. B, D, E: In the quoted verse, Alfred Tennyson uses imagery (b), describing the eagle using wording that evokes sensory impressions for readers, i.e., visual details of its appearance and tactile details of its behavior; alliteration (d), repeating the same sounds across the words *clasps*, *crag*, and *crooked*—the hard /k/ sound complements and reinforces the imagery; and personification (e), giving an animal human qualities by calling the eagle "he" and its talons "hands." This verse does NOT include simile (a), i.e., explicit comparison; or metaphor (c), i.e., implicit comparison.

35. B: This stanza is an example of hyperbole, i.e., deliberate exaggeration to achieve an effect. W. H. Auden describes things that will never happen to emphasize the extent of the speaker's love. Hubris (a) is excessive pride, defined in ancient Greek literature and later continued by Shakespeare and many other authors as a tragic flaw. A hyperbaton (c) manipulates conventional syntax, e.g., "Alone he walked" instead of "He walked alone"—or virtually anything said by *Star Wars* character Yoda. Because choice (b) is correct, choice (d) is incorrect.

36. C: Throughout this epic poem, Henry Wadsworth Longfellow employs trochaic tetrameter (a trochee is /∪, i.e., two syllables, the first stressed, the second unstressed; tetrameter is four beats per line) to evoke for his readers the rhythms of the Native Americans' chanting. Though he asks and answers a series of questions in his Introduction, Longfellow never uses couplets (a), (b); the stanzas vary in length, but are all longer than two lines each. He does not use irony to develop a theme (d).

37. D: Teachers can help students predict what will happen in a text (a) *before* and *during* reading, but *not after* reading because there is nothing left to predict once they have read the whole text. Teachers can help students summarize text content (b) to identify its main ideas (e.g., by previewing text before reading) and identify text-to-self connections (c) to make the material more personally relevant *before, during, and/or after* they read.

38. D: For evaluating a summary of a literary passage, the evaluator should consider whether the student's summary achieved an equal balance of concision and completeness (a); summarized the passage objectively and neutrally, excluding his or her own reactions or opinions (b); covered the passage's points in a similar proportion as the original writer did (c); and tag attributions of ideas to their original authors by name, cite the passage's original source so summary readers can find it, and avoid overusing quotations (d).

39. C: Evidence-based instructional approaches are proven via multiple rigorous research studies sharing consistent results. To evaluate the effectiveness of such approaches as implemented, which teaching practices will be used should be defined in advance (a). Evaluators should establish a monitoring process to assure compliance (b). Student outcomes should be evaluated using appropriate, established measures (c). And student progress with a specific teaching method should be compared to their progress without that method via suitable means (d).

40. A: Research finds instructional strategies that help students use metacognitive processes improve their comprehension and evaluation of what they read. Considering whether they perceive that an author distorts or accurately represents reality helps students evaluate sources and self-monitor their comprehension. Considering whether and to whom they would recommend a text helps them make connections with text (b). Considering intuitively whether a text title interests them helps them evaluate the text, their understanding of it, and their connection to it (c). They should learn to evaluate both author techniques and text effectiveness on its audience (d).

41. A: Literal language, which says just what it means, is analogous to denotation, which is the literal meaning of a word (or its dictionary definition). Figurative language, which adds meanings beyond literal, is analogous to connotation, which refers to the ideas associated with a word beyond its literal definition. These analogies are backwards in (b). They are not incorrect (c), and informational text uses figurative language and connotations (d) as fictional literature does.

42. A, C, D: In these choices, the first noun in each phrase is used figuratively: a mountain (a) to mean a large amount, not a literal mountain; a flood (c) to mean a great many, not a literal deluge of water; and a cascade (d) to mean a series, not a literal waterfall. Choices (b) and (e) both use nouns with literal meanings instead: a plethora (b) means a large amount or an excess, and a series (e) means occurring successively.

43. C: Full reading comprehension of informational text depends not only on remembering important information (a) from it, but also on making inferences based on that information (b). To draw inferences about the information provided in the text, readers must combine it with their previously existing knowledge (d).

44. D: When reading nonfiction expository or informational text, it is most appropriate for the reader to draw inferences about causes and their effects (a), and about problems and their solutions (b). However, inferring what message the author means to send (c) is more appropriate for a nonfiction biographical/autobiographical or persuasive text than an expository one, which is more likely to impart factual information, direction, or instruction than it is to send a message.

45. C: Standards for reading informational texts often include expectations to identify textual evidence, for 8th-graders to differentiate between strong and weak evidence (a), 6th-graders to cite textual evidence to support their inferences and analyses, 7th-graders to identify multiple textual evidence to defend their conclusions (b), 9th- and 10th-graders to cite both strong and thorough textual evidence (c), and for 11th- and 12th-graders to identify things left unclear in a text (d).

46. A: Students must be able to connect informational text they read with their existing knowledge and draw inferences from it in order to not only comprehend the material alone (b), but also to make conclusions AND critical judgments about it (c), as well as their own interpretations of it (d).

47. B: In a paired reading strategy to identify main ideas and details for improving informational text reading comprehension, both students read parts of the text silently rather than reading them aloud (a). Therefore, choices (c) and (d) are both incorrect.

48. B: The active reading strategy called text coding has nothing to do with writing computer code (a). Text monitoring is a synonym for text coding rather than a name for a different strategy (c). The authors cited recommend that, for students to perform text coding, teachers should model it for them (d) one or two codes at a time until students have learned all of the codes.

49. A: In text coding, the code for "I know this" is a check mark. An asterisk (b) is the code for "This is important." The letter "X" (c) is the code for "This is something that I did not expect." An exclamation mark (d) is the code for "This is something that surprises me." Codes like these enable students to identify their comprehension of and response to individual items and parts in a text quickly with concise, standardized symbols.

50. B: That our ancestors created a new nation would go under the main ideas column in the two-column notes active reading strategy, as this is the central idea of the first sentence and paragraph in the speech. Choice (a) would go under the details column as it identifies the time of the main idea. Choices (c) and (d) would also go under the details column as they are each modifiers identifying characteristics of the main idea (how it was conceived and to what it was dedicated).

51. D: Comparing ideas or elements (a) shows their similarities, as does making analogies (b) between them. Contrasting ideas or elements (c) shows their differences. Grouping ideas or elements into categories (d) can show both similarities and differences—similarities among those grouped together in the same category, and differences among the separate categories and their members.

52. C, D, E: In a book of informational text, both a glossary and an index list their entries in alphabetical order (a), and both are typically found at the back of the book (b). Only an index lists the book's main or most important topics (c), and references all page numbers where they are found (d). Only a glossary lists new or technical vocabulary or terminology used in the book and provides definitions of the terms (e) it lists.

53. D: Sentences (a) and (b) use *smart* to indicate the connotation (i.e., implied or inferred meaning) of rude, disrespectful, etc., which readers can determine from sentence context. Sentence (c) uses *smart* for its denotation (i.e., its definition or literal meaning) of showing intelligence, thinking well, behaving sensibly, using good judgment, acting strategically, etc.

54. B, C: Technical language in scientific text should achieve a balance between grandiose (a) and self-deprecating (d) mood, as neither extreme is acceptable (e.g., "Our findings are insignificant" is too self-deprecating, while "Our findings are indisputable" is too grandiose). It should be more impersonal (b) and professional (c) than vernacular or literary language. It should not *always* use passive voice (e), which makes tone more impersonal and avoids first person. Science professors traditionally advocated a passive voice, but today's science editors find it dull and weak, so science writers may alternate active and passive voices.

55. A, C, E: Choice (a) is implicit: the sentence does not directly state she was no longer young; it is implied by "hair... changing from brown to gray." Choice (b) is explicit: "a good strong figure" and "a solid physique" are synonymous. Choice (c) is implicit: readers may infer her "ruddy cheeks" reflected good (blood) circulation. Choice (d) is explicit: "a determined eye" and "She looked determined" both describe appearance only. However, (e) is implicit: readers may infer her "determined eye" reflected personal determination.

56. B: Authors of informational texts do explicitly state their point of view and/or purpose sometimes, but NOT always (a); many authors do not overtly identify it, so readers must infer it (b), which is easier when the author's position is more opinionated, but harder when it is neutral or balanced (c)—or when the text itself is difficult. Therefore, readers have to analyze some text to identify author point of view or purpose, which they should NOT assume indicates poor writing (d).

57. A: An allusion is a reference to something or someone well-known that adds symbolism and/or resonance. A paradox (b) is a seemingly contradictory statement which nevertheless is true. An analogy (c) is a comparison of two different things that share some common elements. A parody (d) is a kind of satire that ridicules a work's subject and/or style through imitation.

58. D: Anticipating objections (a), arguing to refute them, and depicting them as weak support author views by bringing objections up before readers can raise or even think of them. Citing expert opinions (b) supports author views by showing readers that *a knowledgeable authority on the subject* agrees. Bandwagon appeals (c) support author views by showing readers *everybody else* agrees. Testimonials (d)—anecdotes or especially quotations—support author views by showing readers *others* agree (not necessarily an authority or everybody).

59. B: For critically evaluating the effectiveness of an informational text author's methods of appeal to readers, the reader should first identify the thesis, i.e., what the author argues for or against; then consider its content AND why the author chose it (a); consider whether the author offers solutions to problems raised and whether the solutions are realistic (b), which is important (c); and observe not only all central ideas, but also what evidence supports them and the thesis (d).

60. C: Authors who normally write informational text using technical language may have to write using non-technical language for a number of reasons, including for communicating simpler, clearer messages rather than denser content (a); informing colleagues in *other* fields as well as their own (b); procuring funding or support for budgets and/or projects (c); and to inform a *wide* range of citizens of important information they have a right to receive, even *without* having knowledge (d) of subject-specific jargon, terminology, or vocabulary.

61. B: Readers should first identify the conclusion of an argument, and then identify the premises the author gives to support that conclusion—not vice versa (a). However, readers should then list the premises first, followed by the conclusion, rather than listing them in the order of identification (c). They should try to paraphrase the premises, not only to clarify them, but also to make them fit together with the conclusion (d).

62. A: When readers consider why an author wrote an informational text, determining author purpose gives them greater insights to the text, develops their critical reading skills (b), enables readers to know what to expect from the text (c), and enables readers to respond more effectively to the text's purpose and persuasion (d).

63. C: *Post hoc ergo propter hoc* in Latin means "After this, therefore because of this." In other words, whatever happened following this must be caused by this—a fallacy, because chronological sequence does not imply causation any more than correlation (occurring together) does. The fallacy involving introducing an irrelevant distraction (a) is called a red herring. Arguing causation with no evidence of causality, i.e., a non sequitur (b), is the slippery slope fallacy. Refuting a caricature or parody of a claim instead of the actual claim (d) is the straw man fallacy.

64. D: For critically evaluating information delivered through today's multiple media sources, educated consumers should consider (among other things): not only who is/are delivering the message, but why they are delivering it is equally important (a); methods used to capture and

29

retain reader attention, which are relevant (b); point(s) of view represented, which may be even more important than the type of medium (c); and various ways in which a reader could interpret the message (d).

65. B: To evaluate books, readers should consider whether any historical perspectives are applicable (a). To evaluate articles, readers should consider whether the publishing journals include advertising, and if so, for what (b), as this can influence the content. When evaluating books, whether the information is current can be vital for some subjects (c). Finding and reading book reviews can inform user evaluations of books, and author biographical information can inform evaluations of both books and articles (d).

66. D: Repetition—of the same words, phrases, clauses, sounds, images, etc. within one advertisement; and repetition of the same advertising message—are both effective tools of persuasion, as are sentimental appeals. Advertising uses humor to persuade more often than news or advocacy (a). "Weasel words" that qualify whatever they modify often accompany overstated claims (b). Using hyperbole, superlatives, and other intensifiers can also be highly persuasive (c).

67. C: The part of speech that names a person, place, or thing (a) is a noun. The part of speech that names an action or state of being (b) is a verb. An adverb is the part of speech that modifies (describes) a verb, adjective, or another adverb (c). The part of speech that modifies and describes a noun or (another) adjective (d) is an adjective.

68. C: However is a conjunctive adverb (adverb used like a conjunction) connecting independent clauses. A preposition (a) connects nouns, pronouns, noun phrases, and pronoun phrases to other words; in this sentence, to and with are prepositions. A conjunction (b) like and, but, or, nor, etc. connects words, phrases, and clauses. For example, in the rewritten sentence, "I would like to go with you, but I won't have time," but is a conjunction—specifically a coordinating conjunction, connecting independent clauses. A subordinating conjunction (d) introduces a dependent or subordinate clause, connecting it to an independent clause, e.g., "I cannot go with you because I won't have time."

69. C: The error in the sentence is lack of verb tense agreement: "explained" is past tense while "ask" is present tense. Either changing the former to present tense (a) or the latter to past tense (b), but NOT both (c), which would cause the same error only with the tenses reversed. Therefore, option (d) is incorrect.

70. C: Squinting modifier. "Seldom" could describe either "hug" or "are shy." Corrections: "Children who *seldom hug* are shy" OR "Children who hug *are seldom shy.*"

71. A: Lack of parallelism. Corrections: "to stay at home, cook dinner, and *watch* TV" OR "*staying* at home, *cooking* dinner, and watching TV."

72. D: Subject-verb disagreement. Correction: "There *are* a lot of people outside complaining." Sentence 4: split infinitive. Correction: "to shout your answers loudly."

73. B: Split infinitive. Correction: "to shout your answers loudly."

74. B: This sentence has two independent clauses connected by the conjunctive adverb "moreover." The punctuation rule for this is a semicolon after the first independent clause and a comma after "moreover." A very common grammatical error is substituting a comma for the semicolon and omitting the comma after the conjunctive adverb (a). The semicolon and comma's positions are reversed in choice (c). Another very common error is using two commas instead of a semicolon and a comma (d).

75. D: The correct version of this sentence has NO apostrophes. Possessive pronouns like "hers" and "theirs" do NOT use apostrophes (a) like possessive nouns (e.g., "The book's pages") and possessive proper nouns (e.g. "Mary's book") do. Also, "Browns" is a plural proper noun and does NOT use an apostrophe (b), (c).

76. D: Prepositional phrase "as a class" modifies verb "depart," with "as" meaning in the role of (a class). Prepositional phrase "into small groups" (c) modifies verb "split," with "into" meaning becoming or producing (small groups). (Note: Preposition "up" also modifies verb "split," creating the verb phrase "split up.") However, "when we arrive" (b) is not a prepositional phrase but an adverbial dependent clause, modifying the predicate "we will split" by specifying *when*, in the independent clause "we will split up into small groups."

77. A: "Although Ted had an impressive education" is a dependent or subordinate clause, introduced by the subordinating conjunction "Although" and modifying the independent clause "he had little experience working with individuals." The second dependent clause is the relative clause "which made him less effective at relating to them," introduced by the relative pronoun "which" and modifying "he had little experience." Hence there is not just one dependent clause (b), (d), or none (c), nor are there two independent clauses (b), (c).

78. B: A simple (a) sentence is one independent clause. This sentence has a dependent clause ("Every time they visited") and an independent clause ("she got to know him a little bit better.") This defines a complex (b) sentence. A compound (c) sentence includes two independent clauses but no dependent clause. A compound-complex (d) sentence includes two independent clauses and one or more dependent clauses.

79. A: Despite its length, this is a simple sentence—one independent clause, including a compound predicate (entered, walked, sat) modifying the subject (man) and a participial phrase (wearing) with multiple objects (raincoat, hat, shoe). All modifiers are adjectives (tall, black, yellow, red, smallest, other), adverbs (down, alone, farthest), prepositions (away from), prepositional phrases (to the back, at the smallest table, from the staff), and the participial phrase (wearing a black raincoat). It is not complex (b), having no dependent r subordinate clause; not compound (c), having only one independent clause; and not compound-complex (d), having only one independent and no dependent clause.

80. D: The suffix *–ation* commonly forms nouns from verbs, for example, *converse* to *conversation, confront* to *confrontation, revoke* to *revocation,* and *celebrate* to *celebration.* The suffix *–ness* commonly forms nouns from adjectives, for example, *happy* to *happiness, kind* to *kindness,* and *dark* to *darkness.* The suffix *–ity* also forms nouns from adjectives, for example, *formal* to *formality, sensitive* to *sensitivity,* and *gay* to *gaiety.* However, the suffix *–id* commonly forms adjectives from nouns, for example, *candor* to *candid, livor* to *livid, rabies* to *rabid,* and *rigor* to *rigid.*

81. C: Informational writers use definitions (a) as context clues by defining vocabulary they use, e.g., "The Hawaiians ate poi, a paste made from taro root"; words that describe (b) and/or elaborate on other word meanings, e.g., "The obese man's clothes were stretched across his vast expanse of fat, straining almost to burst." Opposites (c) are antonyms of words used, e.g., "Our conversation was very solemn rather than cheerful." Examples (d) illustrate meaning, e.g., "Teachers unfamiliar with ASL may direct deaf students using gestures, like holding a hand up, palm out, meaning "Stop.""

82. B: By observing sentence syntax (structure and word order), readers can nearly always determine what part of speech an unfamiliar word is, e.g., a noun, verb, adjective, adverb, even a conjunction or preposition (albeit not necessarily which one); and sometimes can also determine the meaning of the word. The reverse (a) is not accurate. Both cannot nearly always be determined (c), and the part of speech can be determined more often than sometimes (d).

83. B: Describing a car engine as "greasy" (a) conveys only the *objective*, *neutral* denotation (definition) of the word with no additional connotations. But describing a person's appearance, e.g., "He's got greasy hair, greasy smile" in John Mellencamp's song "Pink Houses" (1983) conveys pejorative connotations. The writing style element of choosing specific words for the associations they trigger is diction. "Gay" in "Deck the Halls" lyrics (c) conveys only the denotation of festive, happy, and jolly; the word acquired another meaning (d) by the 20th century. This is an example of usage, not diction.

84. A: A glossary is a list of specific vocabulary or terminology used in a text with definitions for each word listed. This is the best reference source to find the meanings of technical or subject-specific words used in the text. A dictionary (b) gives the spelling, pronunciation, syllabication, definition, and sometimes examples used in sentences of ALL recognized words in the written language. A style manual (c) tells writers how to organize written works, cite references, etc. A spell checker (d), commonly included in word-processing programs, identifies misspelled or mistyped words in documents.

85. D: Authors portray individual attributes of specific characters by using diction to represent their word choice, grammar, and manner of self-expression. They portray more collective attributes of some characters by using various dialects with distinctive pronunciation, grammatical constructions, and figurative expressions to represent the characters' social class (a), geographic region (b), and cultural background (c).

86. B: This novel is narrated by the titular protagonist, who spoke in the dialect used and lived in its place and time, to remind readers of the setting's significance to the novel and main character. While Frances O'Roark Dowell is from Boone, North Carolina, she did not live in the novel's time period or speak this dialect (a). She did not mean to attract attention with unusual language (c), but to reflect the story's regional and cultural background. She was not creating tension by contrasting dialect with characters (d), but representing the main character's and region's natural speech.

87. A: In Preparation, teachers find which strategies students know and how they can apply them. In Awareness-Raising, teachers make students aware of additional strategies they have not used. In Training, teachers explicitly instruct students in specific learning strategies. In Practice, teachers have students experiment with applying different learning strategies. In Personalization, teachers support student self-assessment of strategy application, transfer of strategies to other contexts, and individual customization of learning.

88. C: According to research from the National Institute of Child Health and Human Development (NICHD, 2000), receptive comprehension vs. expressive production (a), written and printed vocabulary vs. spoken vocabulary (b), and vocabulary depth vs. breadth (d) are all aspects of vocabulary instruction and learning needing further investigation. However, researchers already widely agree without calling for additional study that students must learn not only word definitions, but moreover how words function in different contexts (c).

89. A: Studies evaluating instructional methods for language and vocabulary learning have found that adding multimedia applications to enhance read-alouds and other instruction with grades pre-

K through 2 reduces learning gaps between ELL and other students. However, learning enhancement from adding multimedia was statistically significant for ELLs only, not other students (b). Researchers find children have more difficulty recalling new word pronunciations than meanings, not vice versa (c). They also find that, when teachers add questions and comments about word meanings, children more likely learn those meanings (d).

90. D: Introducing readers to new information (a), explaining to readers how a process functions (b), and developing a concept for readers (c) are all primary functions of informative or explanatory writing. Proving a point to convince readers (d) to believe or agree with the author's position is a primary function of argumentative writing. The former means to inform, the latter to persuade.

91. B: Student skills for locating and selecting information related to their topics from primary and secondary sources (a) involve text-to-text connections. Skills for combining such information with their existing knowledge (b) and experience involve text-to-self connections. Developing writing skills for comparison-contrast (c) and transitioning between points and subtopics (d) is necessary to informative and explanatory writing, but does not involve text connections; citing topic-related scenarios and anecdotes as examples (d) can involve text-to-self, text-to-world, and text-to-text connections.

92. C: Although many people keep private journals to confide and/or process their personal experiences (a) and emotions—in which cases they need not be concerned about their writing mechanics, as only they will ever see them (b)—in other cases, authors write journals they expect or hope to publish someday (c); these do require attention to mechanics and editing. Some authors also write journals for their therapeutic benefits (d).

93. A: Both books are diaries of 20th-century teenage girls. However, while Beatrice Sparks created a fictional plot and characters in her novel using diary format, Anne Frank's diary is nonfiction, written by a real person (b). The fictional Alice develops a somewhat negative perspective on life through her experiences (e.g., she is left with permanent neurological damage), she returns home and hopes for a better life. Anne Frank's entries, on the other hand, convey a markedly positive attitude despite horrific realities (c). The fictional Alice survives; following Frank's last, optimistic entry, an epilogue reports her death soon after (d).

94. B: The Epistles of the New Testament are NOT the only true examples of epistolary writing (a); however, they *are* the earliest examples of epistolary literature. It is documented that, in ancient Egypt, schools for scribes included the epistolary genre in their writing curricula (c). In modern literature, epistolary novels were popularized in the 18th century by Samuel Richardson and continued to be popular through the 19th century (b). Epistolary novels are in the form of letters written in first person by the characters (d).

95. D: An essay's introduction should answer three questions: the subject of the essay (a), how the essay addresses the subject (b), and what the essay will prove (d)—which is the essay's thesis statement. To answer how the essay addresses the subject (b), readers should identify how the author organized the essay (c) through a brief summary of its main points and the evidence offered to support them.

96. C: When writing an essay, experts advise using one paragraph to introduce one main point, present evidence supporting that point, and explain how these relate to the thesis. Each additional main point, its supporting evidence, and their relation to the thesis should occupy a separate paragraph. All main points, accompanying evidence, and their relation to the thesis should NOT be in one long paragraph (a). Neither should writers separate each point, supporting evidence, and relationship to the thesis into different paragraphs (b). Because option (c) is the general rule, option (d) is incorrect.

97. A: Essays with good organization have many benefits, including being more likely to win reader acceptance of the validity of their theses; being more likely to hold reader attention (b); and both being easier for writers to compose, and giving readers better guides for following as they read them (c), (d).

98. B: Readers of reputable newspapers have been accustomed to expecting quality in content, and they usually transfer this expectation to blogs (a). Readers also expect easily readable layouts in print and online alike. However, reading onscreen is harder than on paper, so legibility becomes even more important (b). Also, because readers cannot skim online articles as they do in print (d), but instead must scroll down, blogs require *more* complexity to format and write than newspapers (c), as well as subheadings, graphics, and other text features predicting (b) what follows.

99. D: The purpose of narrative (a) writing is storytelling. Even when authors want to afford insights and/or teach lessons as well as entertain readers, they accomplish their purposes through storytelling. The purposes of expository (b) writing are to inform, explain, and/or direct readers. The purpose of persuasive (c) writing is to convince readers to believe or agree with the author's position and/or argument. The purpose of speculative (d) writing is to encourage readers to explore ideas and potential responses rather than entertain, tell stories, inform, explain, direct, or convince.

100. D: When older students use simpler vocabulary and syntax, and printing instead of script (a), this is an example of writing for certain audiences. When word choice and diction stimulate readers to feel empathy and/or sympathy (b), or to question or challenge opposing viewpoints (c), these are both examples of certain occasions for writing. Writers selecting certain formats, e.g., exposition, persuasion, narration, etc., and kinds of language (d) is an example of writing for certain purposes.

101. C: When students write for their classmates, they should use language that is more informal and age-appropriate, not more sophisticated (a). When requesting additional privileges from parents, students should use language that is not simpler (b) but more sophisticated. When writing for younger children, students should use more vivid and entertaining language (c), including some humor when appropriate. When asking parental permission for more independent activities, students should use language that seems more mature and serious rather than using humor (d).

102. B: Because the tabletop is the largest and most conspicuous part of a table, it corresponds with the analogy of the main idea of an essay or other written composition. Because the legs support the table, they represent the evidence and details that support the top or main idea—not vice versa (a). The table's legs (c) or top (d) do not represent paragraphs, which should separate each main idea, plus its support from another. The analogy visualizes main content components, not their organization.

103. C: Sentences (a), (b), and (d) are examples of information that goes off the point by not supporting the main idea, as none of these indicate a lack of canine intelligence. However, sentence (c) is an example of evidence supporting the main point because it illustrates it by stating the dog does not respond to his name, implying he has not learned to recognize it in five years.

104. A: The sentences within one effective paragraph should all be related to one another and to one main point or idea. Unrelated sentences in a paragraph show poor focus. A paragraph with *too many* ideas also lacks focus; each paragraph should focus on one most important idea (b). Another characteristic of poor focus is *no* transitions between ideas (c). Excessive generalization (d) is a characteristic of poor paragraph development, not poor paragraph focus.

105. D: In the structural paragraph pattern of division (a), a whole is separated into its components by some principle (e.g., steps, body parts, etc.). In narration (b), the paragraph relates a story or part of one, e.g., an anecdote supporting its main idea. In definition (c), the paragraph defines a centrally important term in detail. In description (d), the writer uses specific details, including sensory, in the paragraph to show readers instead of telling them about someone or something.

106. B: Coherent written paragraphs have parts that clearly fit together (a) and flow well from one part to another (b); conceptual content that is expressed in structural patterns that are congruent with the concepts, not contrasting (c); and writer control at the sentence level, which does not undermine but promotes paragraph coherence (d).

107. A: Having sentences unified by integrated, interrelated ideas is a characteristic of a *coherent* written paragraph rather than a *cohesive* one. A cohesive written paragraph has sentences that flow easily from one to another (b); connect old information in one sentence to new information in the next (c); and/or start with old and end with new information, connecting these within one sentence (d).

108. C: A paragraph can be cohesive but not coherent (a) or coherent but not cohesive (b). Hence one does not guarantee the other (d). For example, a paragraph may be cohesive when ideas and words are connected across sentences, yet not coherent when each sentence has a new topic. Alternatively, a paragraph may be coherent when readers can read and understand it, yet not cohesive when sentences are not connected lexically or grammatically.

109. C: To produce writing that is both cohesive and coherent, writers should begin sentences with old or familiar information (a), introducing new information at the end of the sentence or in a new sentence; introduce familiar information by beginning sentences with short, simple phrases (b); make transitions between ideas obvious to readers (c); and maintain consistent topics throughout (d).

110. D: First the writer should narrow down all topics included to a main idea. Then s/he should identify main points supporting that main idea, decide how to sequence those main points, list all the details that support each of the main points, and then organize those details in a chosen sequential order (e.g., by association, by logical progression, from strongest to weakest, or from weakest to strongest).

111. C: Strength and closure are important principles for written conclusions. Readers perceive from a strong conclusion that the main points made were meaningful and important (a), and that the evidence supporting those main points was well-developed (d). Readers perceive from a conclusion that achieves closure that the writer said what was needed, so the work is complete (b), rather than that the writer simply stopped writing upon reaching the required number of words (c).

112. C: The research question or problem statement in a research paper or report identifies the issue under study AND why it is important to the researcher (a); the variables of the study's focus AND why these are important (b); and the scope of the research (c), which is defined by identifying the variables of focus. Therefore, choice (d) is incorrect as it does more than these two things.

113. A: If a source is published in a peer-reviewed scholarly journal, or by a scientific publisher, professional society, or university press with peer review, a source is most often credible. Online publication does NOT mean a source is never credible (b): some are not, but many others are published in peer-reviewed scholarly journals. Author affiliations (c) with universities and institutions do inform online credibility. How many times a source has been cited in other sources also does (d).

114. A: When conducting a literature review, too many references indicate the research question is too broad and thus needs narrowing. Too few indicate the area of investigation and/or research question is/are *too* narrow or specific (b) and thus needs broadening. Zero references, especially on cutting-edge topics, does not necessarily invalidate the topic or question (c); it may not have been investigated yet, thereby requiring systematic searching. Though researchers find more references without planning, they *should* plan searches (d) to avoid getting lost among abundant information which they find interesting, but is not germane.

115. D: For books on paper (a), you must cite author name, editor name where applicable, title, publication date, publisher name, and city. For books published online (b), you must cite the above, plus the URL and access date. For journal articles on paper (c), you must cite author name, title, journal name (or magazine/newspaper name), volume number, issue number, publication date, and article page numbers. For journal articles published online (d), you must cite everything for paper articles (above), plus URL, database name, database publisher name, and access date.

116. B: Although sometimes the choice of style manual is obvious, e.g., English language and literature papers follow MLA style while psychology and sociology papers follow APA style, this is not always the case (a); some professors and instructors prefer Turabian's Chicago style for various subjects. While many professors have a single style preference, not all do (c); in some subjects, some professors allow any of the three major styles. For citing references, each of the three prescribes a different format (d).

117. C: To integrate quotations into research papers, students should NOT summarize each source quoted, disrupting the flow of their own arguments (a); and should keep quotations brief (b), incorporating them into their own original sentences. A seamless way to do this is with parenthetical quotations within sentences (c). Students should be able to use more—NOT fewer—words than their quotations (or at the very least, an equal number) to analyze and concur with or rebut them (d).

118. A: Speakers can establish rapport and personal connection with audiences by making eye contact with all listeners. They can express enthusiasm, emphasize important points, and maintain audience attention by varying their vocal tones (b). They ensure better hearing and comprehension by more listeners by using clear articulation (c). They can clarify and/or emphasize messages and promote audience perceptions of their credibility through body movement (d) and gestures as well as the other components named.

119. C: Available budget is a factor influencing media choices among others (a), including the target audience (b); the duration of a message (d), which not only relates to budget (a) but also which medium is most appropriate for shorter or longer messages, etc.; and, for communications intended to promote social change, the medium's potential for stimulating meaningful audience participation (c).

120. B: If a speaker takes *three* minutes or longer to make a point or answer a question, s/he loses audience attention (a). Moreover, audiences become confused when speakers include too many details and/or anecdotes (b). Because the brain stops processing input that would overload it, speakers should focus on necessary rather than simply interesting information (c) to avoid exceeding audience attention limits. Speakers should NOT avoid or fear pausing before answering questions, which not only allows time to formulate answers but also shows they are thoughtful and controlled, not unprepared (d).

121. D: With digital media, teachers and students alike can use cross-media transformations to convert speech to text and text to speech, including automatically by embedding speech-to-text and text-to-speech software into browsers and other software programs. Choices (a), (b), and (c) are all advantages for diverse students that can be accomplished using HTML and/or XML to change or select fonts and make similar text choices.

122. A: One advantage of web media is instant global access to information. The facts that web media require web designers and managers (b), contributors for content (c), and accessing technical support (d) as needed to address technical issues are all disadvantages of web media.

123. C: Research finds brainstorming effective to help students plan writing (a), and giving students steps to follow in writing argumentation provides the structure they need (b). Collaborative writing develops cooperative learning and social skills while teachers set individual within-group performance expectations and structure; students still practice independently (d). Research also shows that student writing performance improves when teachers give explicit instruction in how to plan, revise, and edit their work (c).

124. A: Mnemonic devices help with remembering information by organizing it into patterns, e.g., rebus-like arrangement of initial letters to form acronyms (like remembering the 12 cranial nerves with "On Old Olympus's Towering Top, A Finn And German Viewed A Hop"). Graphic organizers (b) help with making abstract concepts and relationships visual, e.g., Venn diagrams show both similarities and differences. Making outlines (c) helps with identifying and organizing main ideas and supporting details. Checklists (d) help ensure one has completed all steps or components of a task or project, and with self-analysis and/or self-assessment.

125. B: Research into writing instruction has found that exposing students to writing processes is NOT sufficient (a). Additional teaching techniques are needed, including teacher modeling and think-alouds, which have been found effective (b); providing students with temporary support, gradually fading it as their skills grow, i.e., scaffolding (c); and explicit instruction, found more effective than implicit or embedded instruction (d).

126. A: Rubrics are useful for identifying learning objectives, guiding student work, AND teacher assessment of student work. Teachers should explain a rubric to students before they begin work (b). Then the students should use the rubric components to guide their work (a). Once they have finished, the teachers should use the rubric to assess (c) whether students met all learning objectives included in the rubric. Teachers create or select rubrics to match learning objectives they have identified in their lesson plans, not to organize those lesson plans (d).

127. C: One of the advantages of portfolio assessments is that they can be used as formative assessments (a), summative assessments (b), or both (c). For example, a teacher can review a student's latest writing sample in a portfolio to gauge current performance levels, compare it to the one immediately before it, monitor progress, etc. as formative assessment (a); review all contents of a portfolio collected over an entire school year to assess overall achievement as summative assessment (b); or both (c). Thus option (d) is incorrect.

128. B: The topics of cooperative projects and/or discussions and whether they are age-appropriate in difficulty relate most to cognitive developmental levels, i.e., what they can understand. Social developmental levels (a) relate to whether students can interact effectively in peer groups. Emotional developmental levels (c) relate to student emotional intelligence, i.e., emotional self-management plus sensitivity to, understanding of, and appropriate response to others' emotions. Behavioral developmental levels (d) relate to whether students can regulate their behaviors appropriately within peer groups.

129. D: Research has demonstrated that cultural differences influence human behaviors, not just beliefs (a). To instruct them effectively, teachers need to understand not only cultural differences in students, but individual differences (b) and disabilities (c) in students equally. When teachers acknowledge student cultural differences, they help to keep students from feeling isolated (d).

130. C: To communicate and collaborate effectively with diverse students, parents, and families, teachers need communication skills, including being able to disagree respectfully AND recognize cultural communication differences (a), respecting confidentiality AND being willing to compromise (b), communicating emotions and opinions responsibly (e.g., using "I" statements rather than accusatory "you" statements) rather than proving themselves right (c), and tolerating others' perspectives AND listening to them carefully (d).

131. A, E: To create safe educational environments for students, teachers must create student-teacher relationships based on mutual trust (a), thus choice (b) is incorrect. Teachers must also make sure their students know that they care about them, not only academically (c) or only personally (d), but both academically as students and personally as individuals (e).

Practice Test #2

1. Which of the following works is a short story?

    a. Murder on the Nile
    b. Murder in the Cathedral
    c. The Murder at the Vicarage
    d. The Murders in the Rue Morgue

2. Of the following books, which was published during the Romantic period of English literature?

    a. *Leaves of Grass* by Walt Whitman
    b. *Sense and Sensibility* by Jane Austen
    c. *On the Origin of Species* by Charles Darwin
    d. *Far from the Madding Crowd* by Thomas Hardy

3. Before Charles Darwin published *On the Origin of Species,* which of the following reflected resistance to ideas of evolution like his, based on historical context?

    a. Georges Buffon's earlier suggestions concerning potentially common ancestries of similar species
    b. Georges Cuvier's established proof of extinction from comparing fossils and contemporary bones
    c. Carl Linnaeus's classification and John Ray's taxonomy viewing species as divinely designed and unchanging
    d. Jean-Baptiste Lamarck's theory of environmental adaptation, heredity, and increasing complexity

4. In his *Poetics*, Aristotle defined epic, comic, and tragic poetry genres. Subsequent scholars have altered these somewhat. Which three main poetry genres have they defined?

    a. Epic, lyric, and dramatic poetry
    b. Epic, comic, and tragic poetry
    c. Dramatic, comic, and tragic
    d. Lyric, tragic, and comedic

5. Which of the following accurately describes the most common length, meter, and rhyme scheme of the limerick as a form of poem in the English language?

    a. Five lines; lines 1-2 and 5 iambic-anapestic trimeter, lines 3 and 4 dimeter; AABBA rhyme scheme
    b. Seven lines; lines 1-3 and 7 dactylic tetrameter, lines 4-6 iambic trimeter; ABABABA rhyme scheme
    c. Six lines; lines 1-2 and 5-6 iambic pentameter, lines 3-4 trochaic tetrameter; AABBAA rhyme scheme
    d. Five lines; lines 1-2 and 4 anapestic tetrameter, lines 3 and 5 iambic trimeter; AABBB rhyme scheme

6. Differences in form between the Petrarchan sonnet and Shakespearean sonnet include which of these?

- a. Each sonnet type has a different total number of lines and verses.
- b. One gives a summary at the end, but the other one does not.
- c. Both types end with summaries, but only one provides a turn.
- d. Rhyme schemes, lines per stanza, and stanza numbers differ.

7. In a play, when an actor says something that informs the audience while other characters appear not to hear it, what is the correct terminology for this?

- a. Aside
- b. Soliloquy
- c. Dialogue
- d. Monologue

8. Which of the following classic novels is NOT an example of the picaresque form?

- a. *Tom Jones*
- b. *Don Quixote*
- c. *Daniel Deronda*
- d. *Joseph Andrews*

9. The novel *Pamela* by Samuel Richardson (1740) is an example of which novelistic form?

- a. Sentimental novel
- b. Epistolary novel
- c. Neither (a) nor (b)
- d. Both (a) and (b)

10. What is generally the purpose of the *roman à clef* form in novels and other literature?

- a. To give readers more of a challenge in understanding it
- b. To disguise truths too threatening to state explicitly
- c. To confuse readers deliberately by hiding meanings
- d. To distance readers from traumatic experiences

11. Among the following works of literature, which is a satire?

- a. *Middlemarch* by George Eliot
- b. *Madame Bovary* by Gustave Flaubert
- c. *The Rape of the Lock* by Alexander Pope
- d. *The Red Badge of Courage* by Stephen Crane

12. Of the following sentences, which one uses metaphors to create figurative meanings?

- a. He became a tiger in the boxing ring, but he turned into a pussycat at dinner afterward.
- b. He was like a tiger in the boxing ring, but later during dinner, he was just like a pussycat.
- c. He fought so fiercely in the boxing ring, but afterward at dinner he was gentle and kind.
- d. He was ferocious when he was boxing, but he was sweet and gentle in social situations.

Refer to the following for questions 13-15:

Mamzelle Aurélie possessed a good strong figure, ruddy cheeks, hair that was changing from brown to gray, and a determined eye. She wore a man's hat about the farm and an old blue army overcoat when it was cold, and sometimes top boots.

Copyright © Mometrix Media. You have been licensed one copy of this document for personal use only. Any other reproduction or redistribution is strictly prohibited. All rights reserved. This content is provided for test preparation purposes only and does not imply an endorsement by Mometrix of any particular political, scientific, or religious point of view.

Mamzelle Aurélie had never thought of marrying. She had never been in love. At the age of 20 she had received a proposal, which she had promptly declined, and at the age of 50, she had not yet lived to regret it.

So she was quite alone in the world, except for her dog Ponto, and the negroes who lived in her cabins and worked her crops, and the fowls, a few cows, a couple of mules, her gun (with which she shot chicken-hawks), and her religion.

("Regret" by Kate Chopin)

13. What can the reader infer about the character from reading the passage above?
   a. She was a single lady who was feminine, but also naïve and unrealistic.
   b. She was a handsome, self-reliant woman who valued being in control.
   c. She was a cruel sociopath who was unable to experience any emotion.
   d. She was a shy, impoverished farm worker who did not believe in God.

14. Which textual evidence in the passage provides first an explicit, and then an implicit, foreshadowing of later text not included here?
   a. First the title, and then the word "yet" (paragraph 2)
   b. First the character's name, and then her appearance
   c. First the identification of the gun, and then a religion
   d. First the identification of her farm, and then her age

15. Based on the small excerpt here, what might be a central idea or theme of this story?
   a. A woman will always be lonely without marriage or children.
   b. People who are religious and own guns must be hypocritical.
   c. Strength beats neediness, but one can be too self-sufficient.
   d. Experiencing what one was missing can relieve much regret.

16. Which of the following most accurately describes a theme found in F. Scott Fitzgerald's novel *The Great Gatsby*?
   a. The realization of the American dream through newfound wealth
   b. The corruption of the American dream through excessive wealth
   c. The superiority of those with "old money" over those with "new"
   d. The superiority of the self-made man's wealth over inheritances

17. Of these main themes treated by Fyodor Dostoevsky in *Crime and Punishment*, which one does he explore most extensively and deeply through the largest part of the novel?
   a. The philosophy of nihilism
   b. The notion of a superman
   c. The psychology of a felon
   d. The character's alienation

18. In William Faulkner's short story *A Rose for Emily*, he uses dust throughout as a motif to represent which of the following? Select all choices that apply.
   a. The hiding of secrets
   b. The control of death
   c. The denial of reality
   d. The denial of death
   e. The decay of things

19. One universal theme is that knowledge can be dangerous and destructive to humans. Another universal theme is that humankind is incapable of total knowledge. Which of these works emphasize the first theme rather than the second? Select all choices that apply.

   a. The Old Testament book of Genesis
   b. The Old Testament book of Job
   c. *Moby-Dick* by Herman Melville
   d. *Cat's Cradle* by Kurt Vonnegut
   e. *Frankenstein* by Mary Shelley

20. In Herman Melville's *Moby-Dick,* what is accurate about how the author uses white as a symbol? Select all choices that apply.

   a. He uses white as a symbol of unnatural entities.
   b. He uses white as a symbol of frightening things.
   c. He uses white as a symbol that connotes purity.
   d. He uses white as a symbol of God and the unknowable.
   e. He uses white as a symbol of all colors, or none.

21. Which characters and/or narrators in the following literary works are "frame narrators" who report others' narratives, and also speak in the first person?

   a. Mr. Lockwood in *Wuthering Heights* by Emily Brontë
   b. The narrator of *Heart of Darkness* by Joseph Conrad
   c. Dr. Watson in *Sherlock Holmes* by Arthur Conan Doyle
   d. (a) and (b) are both "frame narrators," but (c) is not

22. Authors Annie Sebold in *The Lovely Bones* and Markus Zusak in *The Book Thief* both use which of these viewpoints or voices to narrate their novels?

   a. The third-person omniscient narrator
   b. The first-person omniscient narrator
   c. The first-person character/narrator
   d. The third-person character/narrator

23. Which of the following statements is most accurate about the second-person narrative voice or point of view?

   a. This is used in literature more often than in informational text.
   b. This is used in literature more often than in popular song lyrics.
   c. With both first and second person, authors can compare them.
   d. With "I" and "you" and a character narrating, it is second person.

24. In which of the following books and book series does the author alternate the narrative voice from first person to third person when describing action scenes, especially those not involving the narrator?

   a. *The Poisonwood Bible* by Barbara Kingsolver
   b. The *Harry Potter* novel series by J. K. Rowling
   c. *A Song of Ice and Fire* by George R. R. Martin
   d. Erin Hunter's *Warriors, Seekers,* and *Survivors*

25. Aristotle wrote in his *Poetics* about parts of a plot structure. His Greek term *peripateia* identified which of the following parts?

    a. The turning point
    b. The complication
    c. The dénouement
    d. The result or end

26. Plot structure must include symmetry to be sound, according to Aristotle. Symmetry can be created through recurring patterns. Which of the following works uses a pattern involving a history of similar events, rather than a pattern of similar behaviors by a character?

    a. "Young Goodman Brown" by Nathaniel Hawthorne
    b. "Bartleby the Scrivener" by Herman Melville
    c. "Barn Burning" by William Faulkner
    d. "Sonny's Blues" by James Baldwin

27. Among the following major types of conflicts typically included in literary plots, which one is classified as an internal conflict?

    a. Man against man
    b. Man against nature
    c. Man against society
    d. Man against himself

28. Which of these is most accurate about functions dialogue can serve in fictional literature?

    a. Dialogue can serve plot advancement but not character development.
    b. Dialogue can serve to illuminate themes and meanings and redirect plots.
    c. Dialogue can serve to set character tone and voice more than motives.
    d. Dialogue can serve to reproduce real speech instead of adding drama.

29. What is true about some ways a reader can analyze character development in literary texts?

    a. Observing differences in what the author vs. other characters say about a character can help.
    b. Observing contradictions in a character's thoughts, words, and deeds cannot inform anything.
    c. Observing the ways in which the author describes each character informs style, nothing else.
    d. Observing the kinds of observations the author makes regarding each character is irrelevant.

30. In literary plot structure, what is correct about the differences between story and discourse?

    a. Discourse is what is produced from the authors' imaginations.
    b. Story is comprised of the words written down by the authors.
    c. Discourse is settings, characters, and events; story arranges them.
    d. Story is what authors invent, while discourse is a story's organization.

31. When composing dialogue in literary fiction, which of these should writers do?

    a. Slow down the story or plot movement through dialogue.
    b. Express their own opinions through character dialogue.
    c. Include only dialogue serving the purposes of the story.
    d. Insert similes or metaphors that show their cleverness.

32. A type of figurative language that uses description to access the reader's senses is known as…

    a. Simile
    b. Imagery
    c. Metaphor
    d. Hyperbole

33. Of the following, which word is NOT an example of the figurative quality of onomatopoeia?

    a. Hum
    b. Click
    c. Buzz
    d. Dog

34. W. H. Auden's poem "As I Walked Out One Evening" (1940) includes this stanza: "'I'll love you till the ocean/Is folded and hung up to dry/And the seven stars go squawking/Like geese about the sky.'" Which figurative literary devices does he use here to emphasize the extent of the speaker's love?

    a. Simile
    b. Metaphor
    c. Both of these
    d. None of the above

35. In his famous poem "The Tyger" (1794), William Blake begins: "Tyger! Tyger! burning bright/In the forests of the night,/What immortal hand or eye/Could frame thy fearful symmetry?" How does William Blake use structure here to contribute to the meaning?

    a. The punctuation matches the meter.
    b. The punctuation contradicts rhythm.
    c. The punctuation foreshadows meter.
    d. The punctuation does (b) and (c), but not (a).

36. Regarding the reading strategy of summarizing text, which of the following is most accurate about what will help students support their reading comprehension?

    a. It will help them to identify important ideas, but not to organize them.
    b. It will help them to identify themes, problems, and solutions in a text.
    c. It will help them to monitor comprehension more than to sequence it.
    d. It will help them to make visual the connections with text they realize.

37. **When evaluating the strength of a prediction on the basis of textual evidence, which of these identifies the best literary analysis supported by the best textual evidence?**
    a. The analysis shows special insight supported by strong, relevant, and accurate evidence.
    b. The analysis shows reasonable understanding with relevant, clear, and accurate evidence.
    c. The analysis shows reasonable understanding and generalized and/or partial evidence.
    d. The analysis shows generalized understanding, including pertinent and accurate evidence.

38. **As a research-based instructional strategy, teachers can have students create KWL charts before, during, and after they read. What specifically does the L in KWL help students do?**
    a. Helps students activate their prior knowledge to construct meaning
    b. Helps students identify foci of new learning according to motivation
    c. Helps students identify what new knowledge they have just gained
    d. Helps students improve comprehension by ignoring prior schemata

39. **Which of these is an example of using a metaphor in informational text?**
    a. Writing that a racehorse ran like the wind
    b. Writing of the cloud of the Great Depression
    c. Writing that a racehorse ran unbelievably fast
    d. Writing of the gloom caused by the Depression

40. **Of the following, which expression that could be found in informational text uses words in a literal sense rather than a figurative one? Select all choices that apply.**
    a. An onslaught of criticism
    b. An avalanche of rumors
    c. A throng of onlookers
    d. A gaggle of women
    e. A belligerent mob

41. **When reading informational text, what is applicable about inferences that readers draw?**
    a. Drawing inferences helps readers to fill in information not stated in the text.
    b. Drawing inferences helps readers answer questions, not understand a text.
    c. Drawing inferences requires knowing text information, not prior knowledge.
    d. Drawing inferences produces subjective rather than objective interpretation.

42. **If someone is reading a nonfiction biography/autobiography, which of these is NOT one of the most suitable inferences that a reader might draw about the text?**
    a. About actions that the subject of the text takes
    b. About the events that are described in the text
    c. About problems and solutions the text presents
    d. About what message the author communicates

43. **For which of the following grades do State Standards for reading informational text expect students to be able to cite and identify textual evidence, and also to identify which ideas or information in a text remain unclear?**
    a. Grades 6 and 7
    b. Grades 8 and 9
    c. Grades 9 and 10
    d. Grades 11 and 12

44. Which of these must students be able to do in order to understand, critically judge, draw conclusions about, and individually interpret informational text that they read?

    a. Locate instead of organize evidence in a text
    b. Organize information without differentiating
    c. Differentiate main ideas from details in a text
    d. Infer about text without any prior knowledge

45. In a paired reading exercise to help students understand informational text that they read, which of the following most accurately describe(s) part(s) of the procedure?

    a. Identifying the main idea of informational text
    b. Identifying both (a) and (c) rather than only (d)
    c. Identifying details which support the main idea
    d. Identifying the main idea and details separately

46. The active reading strategy of text coding or text monitoring involves which of these?

    a. Students make marginal notes in their texts.
    b. Students write text codes on Post-it Notes.
    c. Students may do (a) and/or (b), but not (d).
    d. Students separate codes into two columns.

47. In text coding and text monitoring, which of the following codes means that the student is really confused about something in an informational text?

    a. ??
    b. ?
    c. L
    d. RR

48. Using Abraham Lincoln's Gettysburg Address, students assigned the active reading strategy of two-column notes would place which of these clauses or phrases in which column?

    a. "Testing whether that nation... can long endure" in main ideas column
    b. "Now we are engaged in a great civil war" under the details column
    c. "We come here to dedicate a portion of it" in the details column
    d. "As a final resting place for those who died" in the details column

49. Suppose an informational text on English grammar presents a series of sentences with errors, e.g., lack of subject-verb agreement, and then one or more alternative versions for each that correct or eliminate those errors. Which of these text structures does this most resemble?

    a. Chronological/sequence
    b. Cause-and-effect
    c. Problem-solution
    d. Descriptive

50. In analyzing how the author of a biology text connects and distinguishes among concepts, a teacher helps students identify animals categorized by diet as carnivores, herbivores, or omnivores. Which exercise(s) will help students most to identify author comparison and contrast of categories?

a. Assigning sentence frames
b. Assigning cloze procedures
c. Assigning memorizing terms
d. (a) and (b) will help more than (c)

51. The text feature of boldface is most often used to indicate which of these?

a. A word that has a footnote at the page bottom
b. A word that is listed and defined in the glossary
c. The words of the captions accompanying visuals
d. The words of all text in sidebars on some pages

52. To teach students how to differentiate between denotations and connotations of words in informational texts, what is the best instructional strategy?

a. Sample sentences with multiple-choice meanings
b. Sample sentences using each for the same words
c. Sample sentences that do either or both of these
d. Sample sentences which do neither one of these

53. Among the following hypothetical sentences for a scientific text (e.g., a research journal article), which is/are (an) example(s) of appropriate usage with technical language?

a. "We identified this as a central component of protein metabolism."
b. "This was identified as a central component of protein metabolism."
c. "Fewer than ten reproducible assays make our findings insignificant."
d. "From our findings we conclude everyone needs these supplements."
e. "We conclude that more research is needed to isolate this mechanism."

54. In these professors' descriptions of how some students reacted to administering an assessment in a practicum situation, which would represent implicit rather than explicit meaning in an informational text?

a. "The students, their faces ashen, said, 'We didn't finish giving the test.'"
b. "The students panicked just because they didn't finish giving the test."
c. "The students were unable to finish giving the test in the time allotted."
d. "The students so dreaded breaking protocol that their faces had paled."

55. Which of the following will help readers analyze informational text to identify author point of view or purpose when the author does not state this explicitly?

a. Consider how the author's word choices affect the readers' perceptions of the subject.
b. Disregard what the author wants to persuade readers of and focus on hidden agendas.
c. Consider how strong author choices of examples and facts are, not their effects on readers.
d. Disregard what the author wants to accomplish by writing because only the author knows.

56. **When authors use rhetoric to support their points of view and/or purposes in informational text, by which of these means can they best provide supporting evidence?**
   a. By relating some personal anecdotes
   b. By reporting about some case studies
   c. By making analogies about some ideas
   d. By convincing wording for right and wrong

57. **The phrases "jumbo shrimp" or "deafening silence" are examples of which rhetorical device?**
   a. Hyperbole
   b. Hyperbaton
   c. Oxymoron
   d. Chiasmus

58. **Among author methods of appeal, which of these most persuade readers by making disagreement impossible, so authors can then make them appear to support their positions?**
   a. Generalizations
   b. Rhetorical questions
   c. Transfer and association
   d. Humor ridiculing opponents

59. **Which of these is accurate about what readers should do to facilitate critically evaluating the effectiveness of methods of appeal used by informational text authors?**
   a. Readers should not waste their time trying to paraphrase the text.
   b. Readers should research all unfamiliar subjects and/or vocabulary.
   c. Readers should consider only effects, not which appeals are used.
   d. Readers should evaluate from an author's presumed perspective.

60. **Of the following, which is true about purposes technical writers can serve using non-technical language in some contexts?**
   a. Public surveys of consumer perceptions of science and technology need technical language.
   b. When writing text supporting school science instruction, authors should use technical terms.
   c. Texts on history of science education, popular science, and science and media are technical.
   d. Science authors who also write science fiction must be able to write non-technical language.

61. **Which of these should readers do to evaluate informational text authors' arguments?**
   a. Identify only assumptions that the author has included in the argument.
   b. Word any assumptions identified only from the perspective of a reader.
   c. For deductive reasoning, test if all premises and the conclusion are true.
   d. For inductive reasoning, test whether the argument is valid or is invalid.

62. **Related to the reader's process of identifying author purposes in writing informational text, which of these is correct?**
   a. Stated purposes contradicting other text portions may signal hidden author agendas.
   b. Authors of informational text always state the most important purposes of the text.
   c. The main or central idea of a text means the same thing as the purpose of that text.
   d. Identifying unstated author purposes for texts offers no advantages to the readers.

63. Suppose someone writes an expository essay arguing against legalizing one specific drug, basing this argument on the premise that its legalization will cause all other drugs also to be legalized. What is the rhetorical name of the logical fallacy involved?

a. *Post hoc ergo propter hoc*
b. Slippery slope
c. Red herring
d. Straw man

64. Among others, which of these accurately describes some considerations that educated consumers can apply to evaluate multiple media information sources critically?

a. They should consider only the information in the messages delivered.
b. They should consider author credentials rather than any peer reviews.
c. They should consider target audience, not just publishers and reasons.
d. They should consider evidence and documentation, not simply claims.

65. Which of the following best represents criteria for evaluating websites and web pages as specific types of media sources?

a. Who publishes or sponsors a web page is more important than its domain name.
b. Whether information can be verified supersedes the timeliness of page updates.
c. Before accepting online claims, users must be vigilant for writer and/or publisher bias.
d. Links, citations, and recommendations from reliable sources give no credibility.

66. As an advanced persuasion technique used in the media, what does *ad hominem* signify?

a. "Stacking the deck," i.e., misleading by selectively giving information
b. Bringing up accusations through claiming to deny mentioning them
c. Using majority belief by pointing out that most of the people agree
d. "Shoot the messenger," impugning a message through association

67. The part of speech that most often forms the predicate of a sentence is which of these?

a. Verb
b. Noun
c. Adjective
d. Adverb

68. "She completed the challenging task quickly but carefully." In this sentence, what is an adverb?

a. quickly
b. (a) and (c)
c. carefully
d. challenging

69. "Going to the beach for the day, an enjoyable pastime." This is an example of what grammatical error?

a. There is no error in the sentence.
b. Subject-verb agreement
c. Lack of parallel structure
d. It is a sentence fragment

70. **Identify the grammatical error in the following sentence:**

   She said, "Give it to me quick!"
   a. Dangling participle
   b. Split infinitive
   c. Adjective/adverb confusion
   d. Misplaced modifier

71. **Identify the grammatical error in the following sentence:**

   Growing up in the 60s and 70s, our neighborhood was safe enough to leave our doors unlocked.
   a. Dangling participle
   b. Split infinitive
   c. Adjective/adverb confusion
   d. Misplaced modifier

72. **Identify the grammatical error in the following sentence:**

   Either give it to him or to me.
   a. Dangling participle
   b. Split infinitive
   c. Adjective/adverb confusion
   d. Misplaced modifier

73. **Identify the grammatical error in the following sentence:**

   He found it easier to more efficiently complete the form online.
   a. Dangling participle
   b. Split infinitive
   c. Adjective/adverb confusion
   d. Misplaced modifier

74. **Which of the following sentence versions is mechanically correct?**
   a. You're nametag is in it's place on the table.
   b. Your nametag is in it's place on the table.
   c. You're nametag is in its place on the table.
   d. Your nametag is in its place on the table.

75. **Of the following, which version of the sentence is correct grammatically?**
   a. I had seen her before, but yesterday was the first time I saw her indoors.
   b. I had saw her before, but yesterday was the first time I seen her indoors.
   c. I had seen her before, but yesterday was the first time I seen her indoors.
   d. I had saw her before, but yesterday was the first time I saw her indoors.

76. **"Because he was late, he missed the field trip, and this caused him to fail the class." In this sentence which numbers and kinds of clauses are included?**
   a. One dependent clause and one independent clause
   b. Two dependent clauses and one independent clause
   c. One dependent clause and two independent clauses
   d. Two dependent clauses and two independent clauses

77. Which of the following is a phrase rather than a clause?

   a. He died.
   b. It's raining.
   c. A very good time.
   d. Then we went out.

78. "Bess, who can draw beautifully, loves art; but Grace, who thinks very logically, prefers science." This is an example of which of the following sentence structures?

   a. Compound-complex
   b. Compound
   c. Complex
   d. Simple

79. Of the following versions of this sentence, which one has a complex structure?

   a. You will have to come back tomorrow; you arrived later than the deadline today.
   b. You will have to come back tomorrow since you arrived past the deadline today.
   c. You arrived following the deadline today and will have to come back tomorrow.
   d. You arrived late, which was after the deadline; you must come back tomorrow.

80. Based on vocabulary words you can think of beginning with *trans-*, what does this prefix mean?

   a. Across
   b. Change
   c. Carrying
   d. Different

81. An informational text author writes, "The Native Americans helped the Pilgrims avoid starvation by introducing them to pemmican, cakes of dried lean meat mixed with fat that they made." What is the *best* name for the context clue the author uses to identify the meaning of "pemmican" for readers?

   a. Description
   b. Example
   c. Opposite
   d. Appositive

82. What is applicable about the relationship of syntax to meaning in the following two sentences?

   (1) "The man with a broken arm sat in a chair." (2) "The man sat in a chair with a broken arm."

   a. These both have the same meaning, irrespective of their varying syntaxes.
   b. The syntax in these sentences conveys different meanings in each.
   c. The syntax in these sentences does not make their meanings clear.
   d. These both have different meanings, but not because of syntax.

83. Among figures of speech, which of the following is a simile?

   a. Having butterflies in the stomach
   b. Climbing up the ladder of success
   c. Something being light as a feather
   d. Someone having hit a sales target

84. If a student wants to know the correct form for citing sources that is approved by the Modern Language Association or the American Psychological Association, which reference should s/he consult?

    a. Glossary
    b. Dictionary
    c. Spell checker
    d. Style manual

85. American poet Paul Laurence Dunbar (1872-1906) wrote in which of the following forms of the English language?

    a. In Standard English to disprove the biased notion of black people as illiterate
    b. In Southern US slave dialect to emphasize the cultural background of slavery
    c. In either Standard English or Southern US slave dialect to serve differing purposes
    d. In an idiosyncratic version of the English language used only by this particular poet

86. Which of the following accurately reflects research findings about effective instruction for developing student vocabulary?

    a. To understand specific texts, lessons, and/or subjects, students need direct vocabulary instruction.
    b. To retain newly learned vocabulary words, students need multiple, repeated exposures via drilling.
    c. To increase productive language skills, students need to be taught low-frequency vocabulary words.
    d. To accommodate faster learning, students need vocabulary exercise structures to remain constant.

87. Researchers have found which of these relative to understanding how students learn vocabulary?

    a. Which methods educators use to measure vocabulary knowledge do not matter.
    b. Which vocabulary words teachers are instructing students in must be considered.
    c. Which levels of vocabulary knowledge different students possess is not relevant.
    d. Which vocabulary size variations exist among students cannot inform this subject.

88. In evaluating the effectiveness of different vocabulary teaching methods with young children, what have investigators found about teacher questions?

    a. Children learn new words better when teachers alternate low-demand and high-demand questions.
    b. Children learn new words better when teachers ask them questions without any temporary support.
    c. Children learn new words better when teachers ask them only questions with the highest complexity.
    d. Children learn new words better when teachers scaffold, moving gradually from low to high demand.

89. When evaluating an author's argument in persuasive writing, in which of the following steps would a reader consider whether the author backs up the argument with clear, understandable facts and other supporting evidence?

a. Identifying author assumptions about the topic
b. Evaluating the relative objectivity of the author
c. Identifying types of supporting evidence given
d. Deciding the relevance of supporting evidence

90. Which common mode of writing is most characterized by the author's assumption that certain things are facts or truths?

a. Informative
b. Descriptive
c. Persuasive
d. Narrative

91. Among the following, which is NOT a common purpose for writing in a journal?

a. Documenting experiences with terminal illness
b. Chronicling experiences with addiction recovery
c. Travel to or life in other countries and spiritual journeys
d. Relating the story of a fictional plot and characters

92. Identify the type of letter named in the following:

   Is often published

a. Open Letter
b. Letter to the Editor
c. Business Letter
d. Personal Letter

93. Identify the type of letter named in the following:

   Salutation is punctuated with a colon

a. Open Letter
b. Letter to the Editor
c. Business Letter
d. Personal Letter

94. Identify the type of letter named in the following:

   Return address is visible on published letter

a. Open Letter
b. Letter to the Editor
c. Business Letter
d. Personal Letter

95. Identify the type of letter named in the following:

   Using "Love," as a closing is appropriate

a. Open Letter
b. Letter to the Editor
c. Business Letter
d. Personal Letter

96. Which of the following types of novels are NOT frequently written in the epistolary genre?

a. Epic
b. Tragic
c. Satirical
d. Moralistic

97. Where is the thesis statement of an essay most often found?

a. In the first sentence of the first paragraph
b. In the first sentence of the last paragraph
c. In the last sentence of the first paragraph
d. In the last sentence of the last paragraph

98. Regarding how a writer should address the thesis in an essay, which of these statements is correct?

a. The writer should state the thesis in the introduction and only reiterate it in the conclusion.
b. The writer should clearly restate the thesis in at least one sentence within every paragraph.
c. The writer should explain how each main point relates to the thesis but without restating it.
d. The writer should state the thesis clearly at the beginning and need not repeat it afterward.

99. In composed speeches, which part(s) is/are typically *most* different in content from the corresponding part(s) of written essays?

a. The introduction of the speech
b. The main body of the speech
c. The conclusion of the speech
d. (a) and (c) more than (b)

100. Which of the following reflects a sound principle for writing blog posts?

a. Punctuation is less important online than in print.
b. Paragraphs should be the same length as in print.
c. All blank spaces should be eliminated in any blog.
d. A post should have a beginning, middle, and end.

101. Compared to expository or argumentative writing, what is different about speculative writing?

a. Speculative writing combines information and persuasion of expository and argumentative writing.
b. Speculative writing is less factual than exposition, and less imaginative than persuasion.
c. Speculative writing makes fewer clear or definitive points than expository and argumentative writing.
d. Speculative writing typically uses tighter organization than expository and argumentative writing.

102. Which aspects of writing should teachers help students in considering for choosing content to include and a specific writing format to apply?

a. Considering what knowledge the reading audience has in common with them
b. Considering only the points they can make with which the audience will agree
c. Considering what points to make, which supersedes supporting/proving them
d. Considering information readers know rather than which information to share

103. Of the following, which most accurately reflects how students can use the most appropriate kinds of writing according to their purposes?

    a. Students who want to get readers to agree with them use argumentative writing.
    b. Students who want to tell a story and the lesson it affords use speculative writing.
    c. Students who want to invite readers to explore ideas must use descriptive writing.
    d. Students who want to share an experience with readers can use narrative writing.

104. Regarding writing outlines before writing essays, articles, or papers, which of these is true?

    a. Outlining is a beneficial process for writing students but is not necessary for authors.
    b. Outlining facilitates identifying the main point and supporting details quickly.
    c. Outlining is best for writers to plan compositions, not for readers to analyze.
    d. Outlining should use several sentences each to sum up the main idea and support.

105. Among these phrases that writers often use to introduce series of details supporting the main point, which is best for indicating additional supporting details or examples *after* the first *two* instances?

    a. *Also, in addition, besides, additionally, another*
    b. *Lastly, last but not least; finally; one more thing*
    c. *For example, first of all, firstly, for instance*
    d. *Moreover; furthermore; not only that, but also*

106. Of the following, which most accurately describes characteristics of written paragraphs with inadequate development?

    a. These paragraphs always demonstrate poor writing.
    b. These paragraphs still include required information.
    c. These paragraphs are never convincing or effective.
    d. These paragraphs offer background, which bores readers.

107. In writing paragraphs, which structural pattern most often uses a chronological sequence?

    a. Compare-contrast
    b. Cause-effect
    c. Analogy
    d. Process

108. Among techniques that writers can use to promote coherence in written paragraphs, which one most reinforces the importance of certain ideas?

    a. Transition
    b. Repetition
    c. Parallelism
    d. Consistency

109. For writing cohesive paragraphs, what is most accurate about using the passive voice?

    a. Avoiding the passive voice applies here as elsewhere.
    b. Using passive voice can sometimes facilitate cohesion.
    c. It can serve cohesion by repetition but not old-to-new.
    d. It can serve cohesion by old-to-new but not repetition.

110. Which of these is true about coherent paragraph writing?
   a. Readers are more comfortable when a sentence series indicates paragraph meaning.
   b. Readers are more comfortable when a sentence topic appears later in the sentence.
   c. Readers can identify sentence topics readily, but not necessarily how these combine.
   d. Readers can identify how ideas are connected rather than individual sentence topics.

111. Of the following, which correctly defines an aspect of linguistic form in writing?
   a. Linguistic form communicates figurative meanings for words and sentences.
   b. Linguistic form consists of different ways to encode the meanings of words.
   c. Linguistic form derives from phonology, morphology, syntax, and semantics.
   d. Linguistic form communicates the author's viewpoint, attitude, and feelings.

112. What correctly identifies an example of how writers develop the body of a written essay or other composition?
   a. Writers will often argue for the credibility of their thesis in the body.
   b. Terms are defined in an introduction instead of clarified in the body.
   c. Inductive reasoning draws specific conclusions from generalizations.
   d. Deductive reasoning makes generalizations regarding specific cases.

113. When writing the conclusions of essays, which of these should a writer do?
   a. Write conclusions that introduce one completely new idea.
   b. Write conclusions starting, "In conclusion" or "To summarize."
   c. Write conclusions that apologize for their opinions or writing.
   d. Write conclusions that do not always summarize the essay.

114. Which of the following is an accurate statement about a literature review relative to any research paper?
   a. It is a valuable but optional part of a research project.
   b. It involves reviewing only primary sources of research.
   c. It should be conducted by professionals, not students.
   d. It tests research questions related to existing findings.

115. Considerations for evaluating the credibility of a text as a research source are best reflected by which of these?
   a. The text must be equally current, regardless of the discipline.
   b. The text targeting a scholarly audience offers a bibliography.
   c. The text's value and relevance can be judged from just itself.
   d. The text's use as a primary or secondary source is not relevant.

116. As a researcher, when should you broaden your research topic upon searching the existing literature?
   a. When your search reveals too many results
   b. When your search reveals no results at all
   c. When your search reveals too few results
   d. When your search has been systematic

117. If you are writing a research paper on an English literature topic, which reference style should you follow?

   a. The MLA style manual
   b. The APA style manual
   c. The Chicago style manual
   d. More information needed

118. Which of these is true about the MLA, APA, and Chicago style manuals relative to citing papers, electronic journals, magazine articles, and websites?

   a. They all punctuate and order periodicals citations differently.
   b. They all punctuate the titles of journal articles the same way.
   c. They all order periodicals information in the same sequence.
   d. They all require bibliographies to include names of websites.

119. What is good advice about quoting sources for students writing research papers?

   a. Quote lengthier text segments to avoid taking them out of context.
   b. Write more about the authoritative source quoted than your ideas.
   c. Quote only sources supporting your thesis to convince the readers.
   d. Offering opposing viewpoints gains more agreement than just one.

120. Concerning how to deliver speeches effectively, which statement is correct?

   a. Speakers should avoid practicing speeches to appear spontaneous.
   b. Verbal and nonverbal communication should seem equally natural.
   c. Content communicated is more important than a speaker's posture.
   d. Speakers can sustain audience attention using random movements.

121. When considering the best medium for communicating ideas, which of these is true about TV and radio as two types of media?

   a. TV is a high-status mass medium, radio is not.
   b. TV and radio have broad audience reach.
   c. TV and radio raise awareness, interest, and excitement.
   d. TV and radio only reach the general public.

122. To present information clearly in a written speech, which of these applies?

   a. A speechwriter need not define the purpose of a speech beforehand.
   b. To interest audiences, speeches should not be organized too logically.
   c. Making an outline of a speech first will result in a more boring speech.
   d. Sentence structure and word choice precision must rival reading text.

123. Among these educational advantages of networking using digital media, which is most closely connected to reflecting individual differences among students?

   a. Rapid navigation among multiple media
   b. More diverse formats and experiences
   c. Constant or frequent real-time updates
   d. Global access to information and people

124. Technology-based strategies that can enhance comprehension of communication needs and objectives include mobile phones and text messaging using computers, tablets, and smartphones. Which of the following is one disadvantage of mobile and text media?

a. Cost
b. Reach
c. Popularity
d. Length limits

125. Which of the following research-based strategies or approaches for writing instruction is characterized by setting clear writing goals, observing concrete data, and applying learning to written composition?

a. Prewriting strategies
b. Modeling strategies
c. Inquiry strategies
d. Process writing

126. What has research found about teaching cognitive strategies to help students develop their written composition skills?

a. Teaching cognitive strategies is limited by students' ages.
b. Teaching cognitive strategies is limited by student ability.
c. Teaching cognitive strategies is limited by both of these.
d. Teaching cognitive strategies is limited by neither one.

127. Research studies reveal that teaching self-regulation skills to students improves their writing skills. What is true about this relationship?

a. Teaching self-regulation makes students' writing efforts less strategic and more natural.
b. Teaching self-regulation improves self-awareness of writing strengths and weaknesses.
c. Teaching self-regulation makes student emotions, thoughts, and behaviors disinhibited.
d. Teaching self-regulation enables self-management rather than adaptation of strategies.

128. Among formative and summative assessments that teachers can use to evaluate student writing skills and progress, which are both LEAST suitable for grading student work and MOST suitable for giving students useful feedback?

a. Observational checklists
b. Portfolio assessments
c. Anecdotal records
d. Running records

129. In research-based approaches to assessment, in which learning area do teachers require students to recall information, comprehend it, and restate it using their own terms?

a. Thinking skills
b. Verbal knowledge
c. Scientific inquiry skills
d. Procedural knowledge

130. Teachers must establish clear ground rules before initiating class or group discussions to ensure they actively listen and productively participate. Which of the following rules is *more* applicable to young children and students with behavior disorders than to all students equally?

    a. The rule of not participating in cross-talk
    b. The rule of not interrupting those talking
    c. The rule of not monopolizing discussions
    d. The rule of not hitting, kicking, biting, etc.

131. To respond to all students' individual and group identities and needs in inclusive educational programs, what must teachers do?

    a. Teachers must meet student needs rather than parent/family needs.
    b. Teachers must meet student needs but not express their own needs.
    c. Teachers must meet their own needs through team problem-solving.
    d. Teachers must meet their own needs through independent solutions.

132. Which of these is a correct concept for teachers to explain to students about fairness and equality in creating safe educational environments for them? Select all choices that apply.

    a. Fairness and equality both mean the same thing.
    b. Fairness and equality mean two different things.
    c. Fairness means that each student deserves help.
    d. Fairness means needed help differs by student.
    e. Fairness means providing different help equally.

133. As part of creating safe educational environments, teachers must form mutually trusting relationships with students. How do they impart to students the knowledge that their teachers care about them, both as learners and as individuals?

    a. Things teachers believe have no influence on this knowledge for students.
    b. How teachers communicate beliefs, attitudes, and expectations is a factor.
    c. The attitudes teachers have exercise more influence than their beliefs will.
    d. Teacher performance expectations are the only factors in determining this.

Answer Key and Explanations

1. D: "The Murders in the Rue Morgue" is an 1841 short story by Edgar Allan Poe, considered the first modern detective story. *Murder on the Nile* (a) is a 1944 play by Agatha Christie. *Murder in the Cathedral* (b) is a 1935 play in verse by T. S. Eliot. *The Murder at the Vicarage* (c) is Christie's first detective novel featuring amateur sleuth Jane Marple, featured earlier in short stories.

2. B: Jane Austen's novel (1811) was written during the Romantic period of English literature (1798-1832). Walt Whitman's (1855) book of poetry (a), Charles Darwin's (1859) nonfiction scientific work (c), and Thomas Hardy's (1874) novel (d) were all written during the Victorian period of English literature (1832-1870).

3. C: Before Charles Darwin published *On the Origin of Species* (1859), Georges Buffon suggested (1766) some similar-looking animal species could share common ancestries, supporting ideas of evolution (a). Georges Cuvier's paleontology research found fossils of past species resembling modern animal versions (1799), proving extinction (b) and supporting functional adaptation. Jean-Baptiste Lamarck's (1809) theory that life forms adapted to environments, inherited adaptations, and developed increasing complexity (d) supported Darwin's ideas. Carl Linnaeus (1735) and John Ray's (1686-1691) work showed resistance to ideas of evolution, reflecting the Royal Society's post-English Civil War (1642-1651) reaction—both against science threatening stability, and for science maintaining it.

4. A: Departing from Aristotle's ancient Greek definition (which included being sung, accompanied by a lyre, and having a specific meter), lyric poetry has a contemporary meaning of expressing feelings, while epic and dramatic poetry retain more similar meanings. These are three main poetry genres defined by aestheticians later than Aristotle. They define dramatic poetry (a), (c) as containing the subgenres of comic or comedic poetry and tragic poetry (b), (c), (d).

5. A: This is the most common form of limerick—a short, typically humorous, often bawdy poem. The meters included in these choices are: iamb is weak-STRONG, trochee is STRONG-weak, dactyl is STRONG-weak-weak, and anapest is weak-weak-STRONG. Trimeter is three beats (strong/stressed syllables) per line, dimeter is two beats per line, tetrameter is four beats per line, and pentameter is five beats per line.

6. D: All sonnets always total 14 lines (a). Petrarchan sonnets summarize or answer the first eight lines (the octet) in the last six lines (the sestet); Shakespearean sonnets summarize or answer the first 12 lines in the final couplet (b). Both show a turn or change (c): in the Petrarchan, the *volta*/turn between verses eight and nine sets up the sestet; in the Shakespearean, frequently a sharp contrast of the final couplet to the rest constitutes a turn/change. Petrarchan sonnets have one eight-line and one six-line stanza, and an ABBA, ABBA, CDECDE, or CDCDCD rhyme scheme; Shakespearean sonnets have three quatrains or four-line stanzas and one couplet, and an ABAB, CDCD, EFEF, or GG rhyme scheme (d).

7. A: When an actor in a play says something to inform the audience which the other characters do not hear, this is called an aside. A soliloquy (b) is when an actor speaks a longer piece of dialogue alone. A monologue (c) is a synonym for a soliloquy. A dialogue (d) is a conversation between or among two or more characters; the term dialogue (without the article) also refers to speech within plays overall, but a speech by a single character is never called *a* dialogue.

8. C: *Tom Jones* (a) by Henry Fielding (1749) is an example of a picaresque novel, which tell episodic stories of a roguish main character. So are Miguel de Cervantes' *Don Quixote* (1615) and Fielding's *Joseph Andrews* (1742). However, *Daniel Deronda* (c) by George Eliot (1876) is a psychological novel, which explores its characters' motivations and relationships.

9. D: In *Pamela,* Samuel Richardson portrayed emotional love, demonstrating Romantic influence in the form of the sentimental novel (a). He also composed it in the form of letters, mostly written by the titular main character, greatly popularizing the form of the epistolary novel (b). Therefore option (c) is incorrect, as *Pamela* is both a sentimental love novel and an epistolary novel.

10. B: The *roman à clef,* French for "novel with a key," tells a story readers cannot fully understand without the "key" explaining some elements and details. The purpose is to disguise truths too threatening to state explicitly, not to challenge readers (a) or deliberately confuse them (c). In addition to self-expression and creating art, another main motivation of writers is to communicate. Writing of painful personal experiences (even in disguise) can give authors catharsis, but the purpose of the *roman à clef* is not to gain distance from them (d), but express them while avoiding serious repercussions.

11. C: Alexander Pope's long poem is well-known as a satire of 18th-century English society. The other three choices are all 19th-century novels that exemplify the genre of literary realism, which neither satirizes nor romanticizes its settings, plots, characters, or situations, but depicts them as closely to real life as possible.

12. A: This sentence uses two metaphors (implied comparisons): "He became a tiger" and "he turned into a pussycat." These give readers more understanding of the subject "he" by comparing his qualities, characteristics, and/or behaviors to those of more familiar examples—in this case, to contrasting salient qualities of two different members of the same felid family. Sentence (b) also makes this comparison using figurative language, but with similes (explicit comparisons) instead of metaphors. Sentences (c) and (d) both use literal meanings rather than figurative ones.

13. B: From the explicit description of her powerful build, red cheeks, and determined gaze, readers can infer these features reflected a vigorous, resolute personality. This description, and that of her farm outerwear, do not imply she was feminine; nothing suggests she was naïve or unrealistic (a). Never having been in love and having declined a marriage proposal do not suggest she was cruel or emotionless (c), but prized maintaining control (b). From three brief paragraphs, readers can tell she was not shy; as a farm owner, not a worker, was likely not impoverished; and was religious (d).

14. A: The title explicitly foreshadows in one word; another, "yet," modifies her not regretting her youthful decision, more implicitly and subtly foreshadowing: not that at 50 she had *never* lived to regret, or never *would,* but had not *yet* lived to regret it—i.e., regret was still possible. The character's name informs the story's historical, cultural, and social setting; her appearance informs her personality (b). The gun (for shooting chicken-hawks) is a supporting detail of her minimal companionship, as is her religion (c), which also informs her moral character. The farm and her age (d) inform her setting and situation.

15. C: From the title, plus the early statement Mamzelle Aurélie had not yet regretted being alone, readers may predict she will regret it later; however, this is an individual character study, so the sweeping generalization of choice (a) does not apply (some feminists have confused this for Late Chopin's meaning, but she was actually ahead of her time in insights and attitudes regarding marriage). Choice (b) takes an even smaller part of the short excerpt out of context and makes no sense. Choice (c) reflects both the situation's and character's ultimate ambivalence. From the title and foreshadowing, choice (d) reverses the most logical prediction.

16. B: Although earlier in the novel, main character Jay Gatsby would seem to have attained the American dream by going from humble beginnings to acquire significant wealth, by the end of the story it is apparent that where wealth was concerned, F. Scott Fitzgerald's theme was that wealth corrupted the American dream (b) rather than realizing it (a). In his portrayal of the main characters, Fitzgerald did not depict "old money" aristocrats like the Buchanans as superior (c) to self-made "new money" bourgeoisie like Jay Gatsby, or Gatsby as superior to them (d); he showed them all as equally flawed.

17. C: While these are all major themes in the novel, Fyodor Dostoevsky devotes the most space and depth to exploring the psychology of a criminal, including guilt, fear, anxiety, doubt, etc. Raskolnikov's nihilistic philosophy (a) is shown by his disregard for both others' feelings and society's conventions until the redemptive ending. His sense of superiority to society and its laws (b) is seen in his committing murder and as motivating his alienation (d); both are also ended with his redemption through love.

18. A, E: William Faulkner's incorporation of dust represents both how Emily's secrets are hidden from other people; and how Emily, her house, and antebellum Southern traditions are all decaying in the industrializing society following the Civil War. He represents attempting to both control death (b) and deny it (d) through Emily's actions of denying her father's death, and Homer's death after killing him. Faulkner represents a denial of reality (c) through Emily's self-imposed home isolation, ignoring progress, and preserving her bridal bedroom after killing Homer.

19. A, D, E: In Chapter 3 of Genesis (a), God banished Adam and Eve from the Garden of Eden for eating from the Tree of Knowledge. In *Cat's Cradle* (d), though Felix Hoenikker's invention achieved his goal of helping the military, it was dangerous and ultimately destructive to all humanity. In *Frankenstein* (e), Robert Walton's pursuit of knowledge is dangerous, and Victor Frankenstein's pursuit of knowledge is destructive. Job (b) emphasizes that humans cannot know or understand God. *Moby-Dick* (c) emphasizes that humans cannot know or understand everything.

20. A, B, D, E: Narrator/character Ishmael dreads and associates white with unnatural (a) and frightening (b) things like albino creatures, polar animals, and crashing waves. Although white is traditionally associated with purity (c), Herman Melville does NOT use it thus, but reverses the usual connotation. The whale is white and also unknowable by humans, hence it can symbolize God (d). White can represent no color, and/or all colors in the light spectrum (e); likewise, readers can infer Melville's using it to represent no meaning and all meaning, which humans cannot comprehend.

21. D: In *Wuthering Heights* (a), Emily Brontë uses the character Mr. Lockwood as the "frame narrator" to relate narratives from others, as Conrad uses his anonymous narrator in *Heart of Darkness* (b). However, in *Sherlock Holmes* (c), author Sir Arthur Conan Doyle uses the character Dr. Watson as the narrator to relate the stories of Holmes' and his investigations directly, not as a frame narrator.

22. B: Both authors use an unusual narrative voice and viewpoint effectively in these books, i.e., the first-person omniscient narrator. The most common narrative voice or viewpoint is the third-person omniscient narrator (a), who refers to characters in the third person (e.g., "he," "she," "they," etc.) and knows all of the characters' inner thoughts, feelings, and motivations. When the first person ("I," "me," "we," "us") is used, authors more often make a character the narrator (c). When a character narrates in the third person (d), he or she is limited, not omniscient: characters in the story typically cannot know everything about other characters.

23. C: The second-person narrative voice or viewpoint (calling others "you") is most seldom used in literature; it is more common in informational text (a), e.g., user instruction manuals, how-to publications, and popular song lyrics (b). One advantage of combining first and second ("you and "I") is that authors can directly compare the feelings, thoughts, and actions of both (c). When a narrative combines first and second person and a story character narrates (e.g., Edgar Allan Poe's *The Tell-Tale Heart* or Jay McInerney's *Bright Lights, Big City*), it is considered first-person, not second (d).

24. A: In *The Poisonwood Bible,* Barbara Kingsolver alternates a mainly first-person narrative voice to third person when describing significant action scenes, especially when the narrator was not present or involved. In the *Harry Potter* series, J. K. Rowling (b) often uses third person with a limited narrator, but sometimes switches to other story characters as narrators. In *A Song of Ice and Fire,* George R. R. Martin (c) alternates narrative voice to fit different chapters of the books, as do the authors collectively named Erin Hunter in the *Warriors, Seekers,* and *Survivors* series (d).

25. A: Aristotle's *peripateia* meant the turning point, today also called the reversal, climax, or crisis, where complication (b) occurring during the rising action culminates in mid-plot. Aristotle's Greek term for the *dénouement* (c) or falling action was *lusis*, i.e., unraveling. The result or end (d) was called the *catastrophe* in Greek by Aristotle, where resolution is achieved.

26. C: In "Young Goodman Brown" (a), Nathaniel Hawthorne creates a pattern of Brown's repeated efforts to go no farther into the wood; in "Bartleby the Scrivener" (b), Herman Melville creates a pattern of Bartleby's repeated refusals—first to fulfill the lawyer's request, and ultimately to do anything; in "Sonny's Blues" (d), James Baldwin creates a pattern of the brother's ignoring what another says. These are all patterns involving similar behaviors by main characters. In "Barn Burning" (c), William Faulkner creates a pattern involving the history of barn-burning episodes—i.e., of similar events rather than individual character behaviors.

27. D: Among these major types of conflicts found in literary plots, man against man (a), man against nature (b), and man against society (c) are all classified as external conflicts because they involve a struggle between a character and someone or something outside that character. The conflict of man against himself (d) is classified as an internal conflict because it involves an interior struggle within one character.

28. B: Dialogue can: not only advance a story and plot, but also support and inform character development (a); not only illuminate themes and/or meanings in the story, but also change the direction of a plot (b); not only establish story tone, character tone, narrative voice, and/or character voice, but also illuminate character motivations (c) and wishes for readers; and not only reproduce real-life speech patterns authentically, but also add drama (d) to a story via representing conflicts and the actions that ensue from them.

29. A: Some things readers can do to understand literary characters and how authors develop them include observing differences in what the author says about a character vs. what other characters say about him or her (a); observing contradictions in what a character thinks, says, and does (b); observing the ways the author describes each individual character, which informs not only writing style but also how the author develops each character respectively (c); and observing what kinds of observations the author makes about each character, which is very relevant (d) to how the author wants readers to perceive them differently.

30. D: What authors produce from their imaginations is part of the definition of story, not discourse (a). The words that authors write down are part of the definition of discourse, not story (b). Story includes settings, characters, and events whereas discourse arranges those story elements, not vice versa (c). Thus writers invent the story, and the ways in which they then organize it are discourse (d).

31. C: When composing fictional dialogue, writers should NOT let that dialogue slow down the movement of the story or plot (a), use the dialogue for expressing their own opinions (b) instead of those of the characters speaking, or self-consciously insert similes or metaphors to show how clever they are as writers (d); these are unnatural in real conversation and will read awkwardly in written dialogue. However, all dialogue SHOULD serve the story's purpose(s), rather than be irrelevant conversations in quotation marks.

32. B: Imagery is description accessing readers' senses so they feel they are experiencing what is described; e.g., in his long poem *The Waste Land,* T. S. Eliot conveys a civilization's decay through images of dried-up wells, crumbling towers, and toppled tombstones. A simile (a) is an explicit comparison using "like" or "as," etc., e.g. Wordsworth's "I wandered lonely as a cloud" in "Daffodils." A metaphor (c) is an implicit comparison, e.g., Longfellow's "O Ship of State." Hyperbole (d) deliberately exaggerates for effect, e.g., Mark Twain's "I... could have hung my hat on my eyes, they stuck out so far."

33. D: Onomatopoeia refers to words that sound like what they represent. For example, the word *hum* (a) resembles the sound people or things make when they hum. *Click* (b) replicates the sound effect that it identifies. *Buzz* (c), like *hum,* contains phonemes similar to the sounds made by bees, buzzers, etc. However, *dog* (d), a noun naming a specific animal subspecies, is not onomatopoetic (although words for its vocalizations, e.g., "bow-wow," "arf," "woof," etc. are).

34. C: W. H. Auden uses a simile (a), i.e., an explicit comparison, when the speaker says, "the seven stars go squawking/Like geese," which directly compares the stars to geese using the word *like*. He also uses a metaphor (b), i.e., an implicit comparison, when the speaker says, "till the ocean/Is folded and hung up to dry," which indirectly compares the ocean to an article of laundry. Because choice (c) is correct, choice (d) is incorrect.

35. D: Punctuation does NOT match meter (a) in these verses; it both contradicts the regular rhythm (b) and foreshadows a metric change (c). Contrasting with "masculine" or stressed endings of the first three verses, he omits punctuation between "bright" and "In," and "eye" in "Could," yet uses a comma after "night." Punctuation is also separate from verse length. The irregular punctuation also foreshadows the change of meter in this stanza's last line—instead of the previous trochees ((/ᴗ), the last word is a dactyl (/ᴗᴗ), with an unstressed ending. These structural contrasts intensify intrigue.

36. B: When students learn to summarize text, they learn to identify the most important ideas in a text AND organize those ideas in their minds (a); identify the themes, problems, and solutions in the text (b); monitor reading comprehension; AND correctly sequence (c) story events, essay points, etc. Graphic organizers, drawing, and other visuals help students visualize connections more than summarizing (d), a more mental and verbal than visual activity (though such visualization can aid summarization).

37. A: Criteria for evaluating the strength of a prediction based on textual evidence include that the very best analysis shows special insight into a theme, character trait, or change; and that the best evidence to support this insight is strong, relevant, and accurate. Analysis that suffices but is not best shows reasonable understanding supported by relevant, clear, and accurate, if not strong, evidence (b). Analysis only partially meeting criteria shows reasonable understanding, but its supporting evidence is generalized, only partially relevant or accurate (c), or weakly connected. Analysis showing only generalized or vague understanding, even with relevant and accurate supporting evidence (d), is insufficient.

38. C: The KWL in a KWL chart stands for "Know, Want, and Learn." Before reading, students write under "K" what they already know about the subject, helping them activate their prior knowledge to construct meaning (a), improve their reading comprehension by NOT ignoring existing schemata (d), and acquire new information. Under "W," students write what they want to know and learn, helping them identify what new learning to focus on as they read (b). After reading, students write under "L" what they have learned from the text (c).

39. B: This is an example of a metaphor, i.e., an implicit comparison that equates two different things (the Great Depression and a cloud). Option (a) is an example of a simile, i.e., an explicit comparison that equates two different things by using *like* or *as.* Options (c) and (d) are both examples of using literal rather than figurative language, i.e., describing things without comparing them to anything else.

40. A, C, E: An "onslaught" (a) literally means a vigorous attack or onset, as of criticism here. A "throng" (c) literally means a multitude of people or things assembled/crowded together, as of onlookers here. "Belligerent" literally means hostile, and "mob" (e) literally means an unruly crowd. However, "avalanche" (b) literally means a large snow or ice slide; figuratively it means any sudden, overwhelming amount or occurrence, as with rumors here. A "gaggle" (d) literally refers to a flock of geese; figuratively it can be used to describe a group pejoratively, as with women here.

41. A: Authors do not overtly or explicitly state everything in texts, including informational ones; hence readers need to draw inferences to fill in unstated information. Drawing inferences helps readers both to answer more questions about a text and understand it better (b). To make inferences, readers must not only know the information in the text, they must also add it to their prior knowledge (c). Drawing inferences about text can produce subjective or objective interpretations or both (d).

42. C: Some inferences that would be most suitable for a reader to draw about a nonfictional biography or autobiography include regarding the subject's actions and activities (a), events described in the text (b), and the message the author wants to communicate (d). However, inferences about problems and solutions described (c) are more suitable when reading a nonfiction informational or expository text.

43. D: State Standards expect 11th- and 12th-graders not only to cite and identify textual evidence, but also to identify which ideas and information remain unclear in a text. Sixth-graders are expected to cite textual evidence to support their inferences and analyses, and 7th-graders to identify textual evidence to defend their conclusions (a). Eighth-graders are expected to identify strong vs. weak textual evidence, while 9th- and 10th-graders are expected to cite thorough and strong textual evidence (b), (c).

44. C: To understand, critically judge, draw conclusions about, and make their own interpretations of informational text they read, students must be able to locate evidence in a text, organize the information (a), not only organize information but differentiate (b) whether it contains main ideas or details (c), make inferences about the text, and connect it to their prior knowledge (d).

45. B: When students work in pairs to read and identify parts of an informational text to aid their comprehension, they read portions silently and then agree or disagree about, discuss, and arrive at an agreement as to the main idea (a). They then identify details which support that idea (c) rather than identifying them separately (d) without connecting how the details support the main idea. Identifying this relationship is important to reading comprehension.

46. C: In the active reading strategy of text coding or text monitoring, students write preset codes to note their comprehension status in the margins of their texts (a), on Post-it Notes (b), or both (c); however, they do not separate these codes into columns (d), which is a technique used in a different reading strategy called two-column notes.

47. A: Text coding/monitoring (Harvey and Daniels, 2009) uses eight codes for students to annotate informational text they read. Four of those codes are included in these choices. The "??" code (a) means "I am really confused about this part." The "?" code (b) means "I have a question about this part." The "L" code (c) means "I learned something new from this part." And the "RR" code (d) means "I need to reread this part."

48. D: In a two-column notes format, choice (a) would be entered under the details column as it is a detail related to a main idea, which is choice (b). Another central idea is found in choice (c), which should be entered under main ideas rather than details. A detail that is related to and supports that main idea is choice (d), which modifies and describes it.

49. C: The sentences with errors represent problems, while the correct sentences represent solutions. Chronological or sequence (a) structure organizes information from beginning to end in time (or vice versa), or in the order of steps to follow. Cause-and-effect (b) structure organizes information in terms of events, identifying reasons for their occurrence. Descriptive (d) structure either uses sensory imagery to help readers experience the information or informs readers what, who, when, where, and why relative to its subject.

50. D: Giving students sentence frames (a) (e.g., "A _____ is a(n) _____, so..." for students to complete, e.g., "A rabbit is a herbivore, so it eats only plants"; "A frog is a carnivore, so it eats only meat," etc.) will help students analyze author comparison and contrast of categories. Cloze procedures (b) are essentially the same: they present incomplete sentences for students to fill in the blanks. These are more effective than memorizing the terms (c) carnivore, herbivore, and omnivore and their definitions, as students learn meanings accompanied by reasoning processes rather than rote memorization.

51. B: Boldface is a text feature most often used to indicate words that are also listed and defined in the glossary, emphasizing them so students notice them more easily and know they can look up their definitions. A footnote (a) is indicated by a superscript number[1] at the end of the word or sentence, not by **boldface**. Captions (c) below or beside visuals, explaining them, are not in **boldface**. Neither is the text in sidebars (d), i.e., boxes at one side of a page with added information, often in more focus or depth.

52. C: Two equally effective ways to teach students the difference between denotations and connotations are (a) to provide sample sentences, e.g., using the word "challenge" in a sentence and students must choose among (A) easy (B) hard (C) fun (D) needing effort as the meaning, based on sentence context; or (b) to teach the difference by using the same word in different sentence contexts to illustrate positive or negative connotations, e.g., "I rose to the challenge by competing" vs. "The contest was too big a challenge for me to win." Therefore, choice (d) is incorrect.

53. A, B, E: Although science professors traditionally warned science students to avoid using the active voice and the first person (a) in technical writing, most modern editors of science journals and books dislike the weakness and dullness of the passive voice (b); many science journal articles alternate, so either or both are acceptable. Sentence (c) is an example of overly self-deprecating mood, sentence (d) is an example of overly grandiose mood, and sentence (e) is an example of an ideal balance between the two.

54. A: Description (b) explicitly states the students' emotional status and their reason for it, plus indicates via "just because" that they overreacted. Description (c) explicitly states only the objective part of the situation, neither explicitly nor implicitly addressing the students' subjective reaction. Description (d) explicitly states both the students' inward emotion and outward sign of it. Only description (a) implies their inward emotion by describing only the outward sign.

55. A: When informational text authors do not explicitly state their point of view or purpose, readers should ask themselves and try to answer these four things: what the author wants to persuade readers to agree with or believe (b), how the author's word choices affect reader perceptions of the subject matter (a), how author choices of examples and/or facts affect reader perceptions of the subject matter (c), and what the author wanted to accomplish by writing the text (d).

56. B: Reporting findings from case studies is a rhetorical means of providing evidence supporting author purposes, viewpoints, and/or claims in informational text. Relating personal anecdotes (a) is a rhetorical means of giving readers more authentic and accessible examples of points, and of appealing to reader emotions. Making analogies between ideas (c) is a rhetorical means of illuminating points and enabling readers to relate to them more easily. Using wording and description to convince readers what is right or wrong (d) is a rhetorical means of appealing to their moral and/or ethical values.

57. C: An oxymoron combines contrasting, usually contradictory terms to make sense in an unusual, complex way, often enabling deeper exploration of semantics, like "cold fire" or the examples in the question. Hyperbole (a) is unrealistically exaggerated overemphasis for effect. A hyperbaton (b) uses unconventional syntax to add intrigue and complexity. Chiasmus (d) is two parallel yet inverted phrases or clauses (e.g., JFK's "Ask not what your country can do for you; ask what you can do for your country.")

58. A: One method of appeal is using generalizations nobody can disagree with, e.g., "We all want peace, not war." Authors can then make these appear to support more specific related arguments, e.g., to invade or withdraw from another country. Rhetorical questions (b) need no answers but force agreement, e.g., "Wouldn't you rather be paid more than less?" Transfer and association (c) persuade readers through example, e.g., advertising products enjoyed by attractive actors whom audiences would emulate. Humor can relax readers into agreement, but when it ridicules opponents (d) it can backfire, alienating readers not already agreeing.

59. B: Readers *should* paraphrase an informational text, or summarize it or make an outline of it using their own words, to facilitate critically evaluating its effectiveness; research any subjects or vocabulary unfamiliar to them (b); consider which types of appeals the author uses as well as their effects (c); and evaluate how well the author communicates meaning from the *reader's* perspective, not what they presume is the author's perspective (d).

60. D: When technical writers are also able to write in non-technical language, they can produce public consumer surveys of perceptions about science and technology (a); text supporting science instruction in schools (b); text on science education history, popular science history, and science and the media (c); and science fiction, whose reading audience also largely requires non-technical language (d).

61. C: To evaluate arguments in informational text, readers should identify not only assumptions included by the author, but also assumptions the author has omitted but are required for the premises to support the conclusion (a); word unstated assumptions they identify sympathetically from what they perceive as the author' perspective (b); test validity for arguments using deductive reasoning (if all premises and the conclusion are true, it is valid, but if the conclusion can be false, the argument is invalid) (c); and, for arguments using inductive reasoning, test how strongly all true premises support the conclusion (d).

62. A: Although authors may state their purposes for writing informational text, some authors may leave unstated some equally important purposes (b). The main or central idea of a text is what the reader should understand from it, whereas the purpose of that text is why the author wrote it and/or what s/he wants readers to do with its information (c). By identifying unstated author purposes for texts, readers can evaluate text effectiveness better and judge whether they agree or disagree with it and why, which are all advantages (d).

63. B: In rhetoric, *post hoc ergo propter hoc* (a) is a logical fallacy presuming something must be caused by whatever it follows. It is Latin for "After this, therefore because of this." A slippery slope (b) argues cause-and-effect without showing any causal relationship, i.e., a non sequitur. A red herring (c) introduces irrelevant information to distract attention from the actual issue. A straw man (d) refutes a caricature misrepresenting another's argument instead of the real argument.

64. D: As educated consumers, readers of today's multiple forms of media should consider not only the information in the messages delivered, but also what information those messages are missing (a); weigh equally the import of the author's credentials (which should be included in the source) AND whether the source is peer-reviewed (b), i.e., scholarly; *both* who the source's target audience is AND who publishes the source and why they publish it (c); and not only claims made, but also what evidence and documentation support those claims (d).

65. C: When evaluating websites as media sources, readers should pay attention to BOTH who publishes and/or sponsors a web page AND its domain name (a), which can inform them about a site's credibility or biases; BOTH whether information on a website is verifiable, AND how recently it has been updated (b); indications a writer or publisher of a site may be biased (c); and links, citations, and recommendations from reliable sources (e.g., university faculty), which can support a site's credibility (d), accuracy, and quality.

66. D: *Ad hominem* ("against the man" in Latin) equates to "shoot the messenger": as an advanced persuasion technique used in various media, writers and speakers attack the person delivering a message rather than the message itself, but the message is still undermined through association with the maligned messenger. Misleading by giving only partial information selectively (a) is an advanced technique actually called "stacking the deck" (a). Denial (e.g., "I won't mention my opponent's arrest") is another advanced technique (b), as is majority belief (c) (e.g., "Four out of five dentists recommend this brand").

67. A: A verb most often forms the predicate, which indicates an activity or state, including related words. For example, in "She went to the store," "went" is the verb and "to the store" is a prepositional phrase modifying the verb. A noun (b) most often forms the subject, i.e., the agent or experiencer of the predicate (in the preceding example, "She" is the subject). An adjective (c) most often modifies and describes a noun or another adjective. An adverb (d) most often modifies and describes a verb, an adjective, or another adverb.

68. B: Both "quickly" (a) and "carefully" (c) are adverbs in this sentence that modify the verb "completed," describing how she completed the task. "Challenging" (d) is an adjective; it modifies the noun "task," describing what the task was like or one of its characteristics.

69. D: This non-sentence has no predicate, making it a fragment. Thus choice (a) is incorrect. "Going" is a gerund (a verb participle used as a noun) and the sentence subject, not the verb. Replacing the comma with the copula or linking verb "is" (or "was," "will," "can," "could," "would be," etc.) would correct it. An example of lack of parallelism (c) would be "Going to the beach is more enjoyable than to stay home." Correction: either "To go to the beach" and "to stay home" OR "Going to the beach" and "staying home."

70. C: Adjective/adverb confusion. "Quick" is an adjective to modify a noun ("a quick trip") or another adjective. The adverb "quickly" would modify the verb "Give."

71. A: Dangling participle. "Our neighborhood" was NOT growing up, we were. Corrections: "When we were growing up" OR "we found our neighborhood safe enough."

72. D: Misplaced modifier. "Give it either to him or to me," "Either give it to him or give it to me," OR "Give it to either him or me."

73. B: Split infinitive. "He found it easier to complete the form more efficiently online."

74. D: With possessive adjectives, do NOT use an apostrophe: "Your" and "its" are correct. Choice (a) incorrectly adds an apostrophe to both possessive adjectives; choice (b) uses "Your" correctly, but "it's" is incorrect; choice (c) uses "You're" incorrectly but "its" correctly. "You're" and "it's" can ONLY be contractions of "you are" and "it is," respectively.

75. A: The past perfect tense of the verb "to see" is "had seen." The past tense of the verb is "saw." Thus "had saw" (b), (d) and "I seen" (b), (c) are both incorrect constructions. The present perfect tense also uses "seen," e.g., "I have seen her before." However, because the second clause is in the past tense, the first clause should be past perfect to reflect earlier times than yesterday. ("I have seen her before, but today is the first time I see her indoors" would be correct.)

76. C: "Because he was late" is the one dependent clause (a), (c) that cannot stand alone; it is introduced by the subordinating conjunction "Because" and modifies "he missed the field trip," the first independent clause, which could stand alone as a sentence. This is joined by the coordinating conjunction "and" to the second independent clause, "this caused him to fail the class." Hence there is not only one independent clause (a), (b), nor are there two dependent clauses (b), (d).

77. C: Longer sentences are not necessarily clauses, and shorter sentences are not necessarily phrases. A clause can stand alone as a sentence, has a subject and verb, and no subordinating conjunction, relative pronoun, or other subordinating word or phrase making it dependent. Choices (a) and (b) each have a subject and a verb, and are clauses; choice (d) has an adverb, subject, verb, and preposition, and is a clause. However, choice (c) is a noun phrase containing an article, adverb, adjective, and noun, but no verb.

78. A: This is an example of a compound-complex sentence, which combines two independent clauses with one or more dependent clauses. "Bess loves art" is an independent clause, modified by the dependent or subordinate relative clause "who can draw beautifully." "Grace prefers science" is

69

a second independent clause, modified by a second dependent or subordinate relative clause "who thinks very logically." The two independent clauses are joined by the conjunction "but." A compound (b) sentence has two independent clauses but no dependent clauses. A complex (c) sentence has one independent and one dependent clause. A simple (d) sentence is one independent clause.

79. B: Version (a) is compound, i.e., two independent clauses (joined by a semicolon). Version (b) is complex, i.e., one independent clause ("You will have to come back tomorrow") and one dependent clause ("since you arrived past the deadline today") connected and introduced by the subordinating conjunction "since." Version (c) is simple, i.e., one independent clause, including a compound predicate ("arrived" and "will have to come back") but no dependent clause. Version (d) is compound-complex, with two independent clauses ("You arrived late" and "you must come back tomorrow") and one dependent clause ("which was after the deadline").

80. A: The meaning of *trans-* as "across" can be discerned based on vocabulary words like *transport* (carry across), *translate* and *transfer* (both meaning to bear or carry across), *transgender* (across gender), *transition* (crossing or going across), *transduce* (to convert across forms, e.g., of energy), etc. All these share the common prefix meaning of across or from one place or thing to another. One prefix meaning "change" (b) is *meta-* (e.g., metamorphosis). *Port-* as in "portable" means carry (c). A prefix meaning "different" (d) is *hetero-* (e.g., heterosexual, heterogeneous, heterocyclic, heteromorphic).

81. D: An appositive is a defining word or phrase following another word within commas. A description (a) uses words evoking imagery or sensory impressions to define word meaning, e.g., "The taste of the medication must have been *repugnant* from the way the child grimaced and shuddered." An example (b) would supply some instance demonstrating word meaning, e.g., "The teacher not knowing ASL gave deaf students directions using *gestures*, like curling a finger toward herself to mean 'come here.'" An opposite (c) would be an antonym, e.g., "She had difficulty adjusting to her new family's *laxity* after the foster parents' strictness."

82. B: These two sentences do NOT both have the same meaning (a): sentence (1) means the man's arm was broken, while sentence (2) means the chair's arm was broken. Their respective meanings ARE clear (c) due to their respective word order, so option (d) is incorrect.

83. C: "Light as a feather" is a simile, an explicit comparison using "like" or "as." The others are all metaphors, implicit comparisons without "like" or "as," simply referring to something as something else. These are all figures of speech because the meanings are not literal: the stomach has a fluttery feeling, not actual butterflies (a); one does not climb an actual ladder to success (b); the lightweight thing or person does not match a feather's weight (c); meeting a sales quota does not involve physically shooting or hitting a target (d).

84. D: A glossary (a) within a specific text gives definitions for selected words used in the text that are technical, discipline-specific, or otherwise specialized or uncommon. A dictionary (b) gives definitions, pronunciation, and sometimes examples in sentences for all recognized words in the written language. A spell checker (c) is a function typically built into word-processing programs to detect misspelled or mistyped words in documents users create. The MLA, APA, and Kate Turabian (Chicago) define different styles of formatting and citation in academic publications: a style manual (d) is the best reference for citing sources in a chosen style.

85. C: Paul Laurence Dunbar wrote some poems in Standard English, e.g., "We Wear the Mask" about how black people could not reveal their true thoughts and feelings to the white establishment; and some in Southern US slave dialect, e.g., "When Malindy Sings" to reflect the cultural backgrounds of American slaves. He did not write in only one (a) or the other (b), nor did he use any individually unique version of English (d).

86. A: Research from the National Reading Technical Assistance Center (NRTAC, 2010) finds the following: Because children often must learn specific word meanings to understand texts, lessons, and/or subjects, teachers must give them direct instruction in the vocabulary words involved. To retain newly acquired vocabulary words, students need repeated exposures in varied contexts, NOT via drilling (b). To increase productive language skills, students need to be taught *high*-frequency words they can apply in many contexts (c). When students understand task expectations, they frequently learn faster; hence teachers should restructure vocabulary exercises as needed (d).

87. B: Researchers from the National Institute of Child Health and Human Development (NICHD) report that, to understand how students learn vocabulary, it is necessary to consider which methods educators use to measure vocabulary knowledge (a), in which vocabulary words teachers are instructing students (b), levels of student vocabulary knowledge (c), and variations in vocabulary size among students (d).

88. D: Investigators evaluating teacher questioning and support techniques find that young children learn new words better when teachers provide scaffolding (i.e., temporary support, provided as needed and gradually withdrawn as proficiency increases) by starting with low-demand questions and gradually adding complexity until questions become high-demand, rather than alternating between low and high demand (a), not providing any scaffolding (b), or asking only high-demand questions (c).

89. B: Identifying author assumptions, i.e., things the author accepts without proof, can keep readers from being misled by inaccurate or illogical assumptions producing flawed arguments; this does not involve considering supporting evidence. However, evaluating how objective the author is (b) does involve how clear and understandable the evidence s/he presents is. Research results, case studies, personal observations and experiences, facts, expert testimony and opinions, examples, comparisons, etc. are types of supporting evidence given (c), not identifying their quality. Deciding evidence relevance (d) involves how directly or closely related it is to the argument, not its clarity.

90. A: A primary characteristic of informative or explanatory writing is that the author assumes certain things to be factual or true. From these assumptions, the author proceeds to inform readers, explain things to them, and offer them insights. Descriptive (b) writing uses multiple sensory details to paint a picture for readers so they can feel they are experiencing what is described. Persuasive (c) writing endeavors to convince readers something is true rather than assuming it is. Narrative (d) writing relates a story or stories to readers.

91. D: Common purposes for writing in journals include working through feelings, e.g., grief, for therapeutic reasons; documenting experiences with the writer's or another's terminal illness (a); chronicling experiences with recovery from addiction (b); and describing travels to and/or life in other countries or spiritual journals (c). However, relating stories of fictional plots and characters (d) is commonly achieved through writing novels, novellas, and short stories rather than journals.

92. A, B: Open letters may or may not identify individuals or groups addressed and are meant for publication. Letters to the Editor address editors of newspapers, magazines, or other publications and may often be published. Business and personal letters are not routinely published (though sometimes are, as when written by famous authors). Salutations in personal letters should be punctuated with a comma, and the other three with a colon. Business letters should always show a return address, while personal letters may or may not. However, published letters typically show the writer's name, city, and state but not mailing address. ONLY personal letters should close with "Love" followed by a comma.

93. A, B, C: Open letters may or may not identify individuals or groups addressed and are meant for publication. Letters to the Editor address editors of newspapers, magazines, or other publications and may often be published. Business and personal letters are not routinely published (though sometimes are, as when written by famous authors). Salutations in personal letters should be punctuated with a comma, and the other three with a colon. Business letters should always show a return address, while personal letters may or may not. However, published letters typically show the writer's name, city, and state but not mailing address. ONLY personal letters should close with "Love" followed by a comma.

94. C, D: Open letters may or may not identify individuals or groups addressed and are meant for publication. Letters to the Editor address editors of newspapers, magazines, or other publications and may often be published. Business and personal letters are not routinely published (though sometimes are, as when written by famous authors). Salutations in personal letters should be punctuated with a comma, and the other three with a colon. Business letters should always show a return address, while personal letters may or may not. However, published letters typically show the writer's name, city, and state but not mailing address. ONLY personal letters should close with "Love" followed by a comma.

95. D: Open letters may or may not identify individuals or groups addressed and are meant for publication. Letters to the Editor address editors of newspapers, magazines, or other publications and may often be published. Business and personal letters are not routinely published (though sometimes are, as when written by famous authors). Salutations in personal letters should be punctuated with a comma, and the other three with a colon. Business letters should always show a return address, while personal letters may or may not. However, published letters typically show the writer's name, city, and state but not mailing address. ONLY personal letters should close with "Love" followed by a comma.

96. A: Epics are not generally known to be in epistolary form, i.e., letters written by the characters. However, epistolary novels may be tragic (b), e.g., Johann Wolfgang von Goethe's *The Sorrows of Young Werther* (1774); moralistic (d), e.g., Samuel Richardson's *Pamela, Or Virtue Rewarded* (1740); or satirical, like Henry Fielding's lampoon of *Pamela* entitled *Shamela* (1741). Oliver Goldsmith and Fanny Burney also wrote 18th-century satirical epistolary novels. Gothic novels have also been epistolary, e.g., Mary Shelley's *Frankenstein* (1818) and Bram Stoker's *Dracula* (1897).

97. C: While author preference determines this, the most frequent location for the thesis statement in an essay is the last sentence of the first paragraph. This allows authors to give information establishing the subject and leading to the thesis, yet still state it fairly early in the essay, e.g., the end of the introduction. Students learning essay writing may open with a thesis statement (a), but experienced authors seldom do. Waiting until the beginning (b) or end (d) of the last paragraph before stating the thesis prevents clarifying the message soon enough.

98. B: In essays, a writer should first clearly state the thesis in the essay's introduction, usually by the end of the introductory paragraph. Then, he or she should not only explain how each main idea presented relates to the thesis, but also clearly restate the thesis itself in at least one sentence of every new paragraph (b). Therefore, choices (c) and (d) are both incorrect.

99. D: Speech introductions (a) differ from essay introductions by greeting the audience, naming specific listeners at official functions, naming distinguished guests as applies, the speaker's self-introduction, introducing the topic, and stating the speech's purpose. Speech bodies (b) are very similar to essay bodies in stating main points, elaborating, and providing supporting evidence. Speech conclusions (c) differ from essay conclusions by stating the speaker's hope for accomplishing the purpose identified and thanking the audience for listening; essay conclusions restate introduction content and may summarize body highlights.

100. D: According to experts, punctuation is even *more* important online than in print (a). Beginners are advised to start with shorter sentences. Blog paragraphs should be *much shorter* than print paragraphs (b), like two to six sentences each, because reading online is more difficult. Writers should leave enough blank space (c) because readers' eyes and brains tire from overly busy web pages. Because online readers often approach blog posts in varying orders, bloggers should write consistently throughout each post, telling a story with a beginning, middle, and end (d).

101. C: Speculative writing does not aim either to inform, explain to, or direct readers as expository writing does, nor to persuade readers as argumentative writing does (a). While it is less factual than exposition, it is typically *more* imaginative than argumentation or persuasion (b). Speculation, by its open-ended nature, explores possibilities and stimulates questions rather than asserting answers; as such, it does not make as clear or definitive points as exposition or argument (c). Consistently with this nature, speculative writing tends to use *looser* structures than the other two (d).

102. A: To help students in their selection of content and format when writing, teachers should guide students to consider what knowledge they and their reading audience share in common (a), which points they intend to make that readers will *disagree* with (b), what supporting evidence they will need to supply to support or prove the points they make (c), and what information they need to share with their reading audience (d).

103. A: Students who want to get readers to agree with them should use argumentation or persuasion. Those wanting to relate a story and the lesson to learn from it should use narrative writing (b). Those wanting to invite readers to explore ideas with them should use speculative writing (c). Students wanting to share an experience with readers should use descriptive writing (d) to make it more real.

104. B: Outlining is a beneficial process for professional authors as well as writing students (a) to plan their compositions. It facilitates quickly identifying the main point and supporting details (b) without having to search through a fully developed piece's additional language. It not only helps writers plan, but also helps readers analyze completed written text (c). When outlining, writers and readers should summarize the main idea and number and list its supporting details in only ONE sentence for each (d).

105. D: The phrases in choice (a) are most appropriate to introduce the writer's second supporting detail or piece of evidence. The phrases in choice (b) are best for introducing the last supporting detail. The phrases in choice (c) are indicated for introducing the first piece of supporting evidence.

106. C: Paragraphs that are undeveloped or inadequately developed may still demonstrate good writing (a), but if they often omit information that readers need (b), they are never convincing or effective (c) because they may leave out necessary background that the writer incorrectly assumes readers already know and thus will be bored by its repetition (d). They may also omit setting descriptions, key term definitions, supporting evidence, specific details, contexts for others' ideas, etc.

107. D: Comparison-contrast (a) paragraph structural patterns identify similarities and differences between two or more things. Cause-and-effect (b) patterns identify causes of some occurrence or characteristic, or effects of some causal factors. They may move from cause to effect or from effect to cause, but otherwise do not sequence any series of events chronologically. Analogies (c) compare two things from different categories or are otherwise not usually compared. Process (d) patterns describe or explain some progression, most often in chronological sequence.

108. B: Techniques promoting paragraph coherence include transitions (a), i.e., using words and phrases to connect ideas and sentences; repetition (b), i.e., repeating key words and phrases across sentences to reinforce their importance as well as help sentences flow together; parallelism (c), i.e., using adjacent phrases, clauses, or sentences mirroring the same syntax to make sentence structure consistent; and overall consistency (d), i.e., making point of view, tone, linguistic register, and writing style compatible within and across paragraphs.

109. C: Although teachers often warn students to avoid using the passive voice in their writing, this does not always apply when pursuing paragraph cohesion (a), which using passive voice can sometimes facilitate (b) by enabling both repetition (c) of words or phrases closer together (e.g., at the end of one sentence and the beginning of the next), and also old-to-new (d) presentation of information. For example: "Scientists study <u>black holes</u>. <u>Black holes</u> form when dead stars collapse." These sentences flow together, both by repeating the underlined phrase and by presenting old or known information followed by new.

110. A: Regarding paragraph coherence, readers are more comfortable when a series of sentences indicates the overall paragraph meaning, and when the sentence topic appears *earlier* in the sentence, not later (b). Coherently written paragraphs make it easy for readers to identify not only each individual sentence topic (c), but also how these topics combine into groups of connected ideas (d).

111. C: Linguistic form is derived from the phonology (speech sound system), morphology (individual structural and grammatical units of meaning), syntax (sentence structure and word order), and semantics (vocabulary word meanings). Communicating figurative meanings (a); encoding word meanings in different ways (b); and communicating the author's viewpoint, attitude, and feelings (d) are all aspects and functions of writing style, not linguistic form.

112. A: Writers establish their main idea or thesis in an essay introduction. They then often argue for the credibility of that thesis in the essay body. If a writer has included ambiguous terms in the introduction, s/he may clarify these in the body (b). When writers use inductive reasoning for development, they move from specific to general by giving many specific instances to arrive at some general principle, not vice versa (c). When they use deductive reasoning, they move from general to specific by applying some general principle to conclusions about specific instances, not vice versa (d).

113. D: Students and other beginning writers should NOT introduce a completely new idea in the conclusion of an essay (a); should NOT begin a conclusion with an overly obvious and unoriginal "In conclusion," "To summarize" (b), "In summary," etc.; and should NOT apologize for their opinions and/or writing in the conclusion (c). They SHOULD, however, write conclusions that do not summarize the essay (d), avoiding the pitfall of assuming every conclusion should always be a summary (d).

114. D: A literature review is not optional, but a necessary and essential part of any research project and paper reporting on it (a). It can involve reviewing both primary (original) and secondary (references to primary) sources (b). Not only professionals, but also students (c) should conduct literature reviews to write research papers. Literature reviews show what studies have already been done into one's research questions or problems, and also test those research questions relative to existing findings (d).

115. B: One criterion for evaluating source credibility is currency. However, in some disciplines, rapid research advances outdate extant literature quickly, whereas in others, little significant change occurs for long periods—and anything in between (a). A scholarly target audience means the text will offer a bibliography with additional sources (b). To judge intellectual value and relevance, consult other related sources and those citing the source (c). Use as a primary or secondary source IS relevant (d): some not meeting all scholarly standards can still be useful (d). Primary sources require analysis, while secondary sources may offer theoretical frameworks and/or support arguments.

116. C: When your search reveals far too many results, you should *narrow* your topic (a), not broaden it. When it reveals no results at all (b), the topic may be too new to have been investigated yet; this indicates a more systematic search (d), e.g., periodical abstracts to review literature, then references cited in a specific source. Such searching does NOT indicate need to broaden the topic. Too few results (c) likely indicates you should broaden your topic.

117. A: Research papers on English language and literature topics follow the Modern Language Association or MLA style. Papers on psychology, sociology, and other social sciences follow the American Psychological Association (or APA) style (b). Some professors and instructors prefer Kate Turabian's Chicago style (c) for various topics; if so, they usually specify this in the course syllabus and/or tell classes. Therefore, option (d) is incorrect.

118. A: MLA, APA, and Chicago (Turabian) style manuals all differ in whether they prescribe quotation marks or not around article titles, and in what sequences they order information like article titles, publication names, issue numbers, page numbers, etc. Therefore, options (b) and (c) are both incorrect. All three style manuals do NOT require bibliographies to include website names (d); however, they all advise including website URLS and the dates accessed within a paper's body.

119. D: When writing research papers, students should keep quotations from sources short (a) because long quotations are not the student's own words and constitute padding. Quotations should not inhibit or replace discussion but stimulate it because students should write more about their own ideas to develop these than about sources quoted (b). Rather than only quoting sources supporting their thesis (c), students can enable reasonably skeptical readers to agree with them by presenting both supporting and opposing viewpoints (d).

120. B: Speakers should practice their speeches extensively to ensure confidence and ease of delivery; they will not be received as spontaneous in a good way if they stumble, search for words, stop to consult notes, etc. (a). They should use nonverbal communication to seem as natural as verbal communication (b). Maintaining good posture (c) is important in order to be credible with audiences. Speakers should avoid random or irrelevant movements while speaking, e.g., hair-twirling, foot-tapping, pencil-tapping, face-rubbing, etc., which distract audience attention from speech content (d).

121. C: Both TV and radio are high-status mass media (a), i.e., they reach many people. TV has a broad reach, and radio has a broad-to-medium reach (b). Both can raise awareness, interest, and excitement (c). TV reaches the general public, but also enables messages to be customized for specialized target audiences; radio in general reaches specific target audiences (d). TV also has the obvious advantage over radio of audio plus video, but the disadvantage of costing more.

122. D: For clarity in a written speech, the speechwriter must define the purpose of the speech in advance (a). For audiences to follow it, the speech must be organized logically (b). Making an outline first gives the speechwriter a blueprint to focus and direct the speech to accomplish its purpose (c). Good sentence construction and precise word choice are equally important in speeches as in reading text (d).

123. B: Being able to link digital media and materials and navigate rapidly among them (a) is an advantage to all students, enabling access to many learning supports along with texts they read and study. Timely updates (c) are advantages to both students and teachers for accessing the most current information. Global access to information and people (d) like experts, mentors, and peers is an advantage to students and teachers enabling interconnection of information and communication. More diverse formats and experiences (b) are advantages more closely reflecting the diversity of individual students.

124. D: One disadvantage of mobile and text media is that text messages must be brief. Advantages of mobile and text media include that costs are decreasing (a), reach is increasing (especially in rural areas) (b), and these technologies are highly popular (c). Other disadvantages include charges from providers not offering unlimited text plans, and that these media work best when connected to other communications. However, rapid technology advances may change these.

125. C: Prewriting strategies (a) include helping students generate ideas, organize them, access their background knowledge, identify research topics, and use graphics to visualize ideas. Modeling strategies (b) include teacher demonstration, giving students exemplary models of expected writing types, helping students analyze models, and inviting students to emulate effective model elements in their writing. Process writing (d) includes giving students opportunities for extended practice, peer interaction, personal responsibility, writing for authentic audiences, and self-evaluation. Inquiry strategies (c) include setting clear goals, observing concrete data, and applying learning.

126. D: Multiple research studies have found that teaching cognitive strategies to students helps them with planning, composing, revising, and editing written compositions; this applies to students of all ages (a) and ability levels (b). Therefore, neither variable limits this practice (d), so choice (c) is incorrect.

127. B: Research studies have shown that teaching self-regulation makes student writing efforts *more* strategic (a), better targeting desired results; improves self-awareness of writing strengths and weaknesses (b); enables students to *inhibit* emotions, thoughts, and behaviors better when needed (c); enables self-management; AND empowers students to adapt writing strategies as needed (d).

128. C: Teachers can use observational checklists (a) to show how many of a total a student does correctly (e.g., key parts of their speeches they remember, baskets made out of basketball free throws, steps followed in a science experiment) to give grades; portfolio assessments (b) as both formative and summative assessments to show progress and products, informing grading; and running records (d) to show percentage of words used correctly. Anecdotal records (c) are harder to use for grading, but because they enable recording all pertinent information, they are better for giving students useful feedback.

129. B: To assess thinking skills (a), teachers have students summarize cognitive strategies; identify the best strategies applying to provided scenarios; assign student observation of accurate or inaccurate, responsible or irresponsible, and open- or closed-minded (or narrow-minded) thinking; and assign real-life applications of thinking strategies. To assess scientific inquiry skills (c), teachers provide problems or situations requiring hands on research activities and speculation, investigation, and hypothesis formulation. To assess procedural knowledge (d), teachers have students identify procedures applying to various situations, and their correct use for everyday problems. To assess verbal knowledge (b), teachers have students recall, comprehend, and restate information.

130. D: Good ground rules for teachers to establish before initiating class or group discussions include no cross-talk (a), no interrupting others (b), and no monopolizing the discussion (c), all of which may apply equally to all students. However, the rule prohibiting hitting, kicking, biting (d) or similar aggressive physical contact is more applicable to young children and students with behavior disorders, as these behaviors are not common among all other students.

131. C: In inclusive educational programs, teachers must meet not only student needs, but also the needs of students' parents and families (a); effectively communicate their own needs (b); and be willing to find solutions to their own needs through team-based problem-solving (c) rather than seeking solutions independently (d).

132. B, C, D, E: The only incorrect choice is (a). Students, especially younger ones, may mistakenly equate fairness and equality, but their meanings differ (b) and teachers must explain this. For example, students needing eyeglasses to see cannot be deprived of them because that would be unfair, but making all students wear eyeglasses, even those who do not need them, is also unfair. Hence fairness means every student deserves help equally (c), AND this help differs for different students (d). Thus to be fair, teachers must equally provide all students different kinds of help (e).

133. B: The ways in which teachers make sure that their students know their teachers care about them, both as learners and as individual persons, are through the teachers' own beliefs (a), their attitudes equally (c), their performance expectations for students as well as their beliefs and attitudes (d), and also how they communicate these (b).

Thank You

We at Mometrix would like to extend our heartfelt thanks to you, our friend and patron, for allowing us to play a part in your journey. It is a privilege to serve people from all walks of life who are unified in their commitment to building the best future they can for themselves.

The preparation you devote to these important testing milestones may be the most valuable educational opportunity you have for making a real difference in your life. We encourage you to put your heart into it—that feeling of succeeding, overcoming, and yes, conquering will be well worth the hours you've invested.

We want to hear your story, your struggles and your successes, and if you see any opportunities for us to improve our materials so we can help others even more effectively in the future, please share that with us as well. **The team at Mometrix would be absolutely thrilled to hear from you!** So please, send us an email (support@mometrix.com) and let's stay in touch.

If you feel as though you need additional help, please check out the other resources we offer:

Study Guide: http://MometrixStudyGuides.com/FTCE

Flashcards: http://MometrixFlashcards.com/FTCE